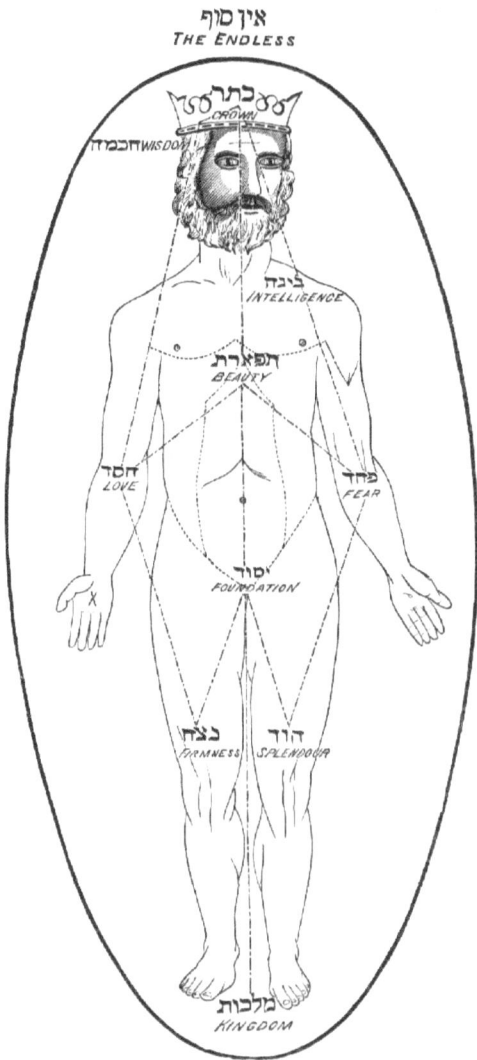

Adam Kadmon or "The Grand Man"

By Signs and Symbols

Initiation in the Western Mystery Tradition

By Dr. Paul A. Clark

Steward of The Fraternity of the Hidden Light

© *2016 Paul A. Clark*

All rights reserved. No part of this book may be reproduced or utilized in any way, electronic or mechanical, including photocopying, recording, or by any information storage and retrieval system, without permission in writing from the publisher.

Edited by Judith Ostrowitz, Ph.D.

"To deny the Mind's creative power is to reduce a person to utter helplessness"

- James Randolph Price, <u>The Alchemist's Handbook</u>, 2000. Carlsbad, Ca.: Hay House, Inc.

Preface

We live in a new age, facing new challenges, new ordeals. We are poised on the threshold of forever facing a future of infinite possibilities. But such has been the case for sincere aspirants to initiation since the times of the misty beginnings. In eras past our brothers and sisters made great sacrifices and faced many dangers in order to seek the Pearl of Great Price. Many of them traveled long distances, across sea, desert and mountains. In those days one did not simply book passage on the Internet and travel in comfort with the only concern being a good restaurant or convenient location for a hotel.

At this time, human culture is undergoing a global spiritual awakening. More and more, the breach between the exoteric and esoteric sciences that occurred 600 years ago is being healed. The separation of human civilization from the natural environment led to the rape of Mother Earth, but is now in the process of being replaced by a more vigilant return to a true partnership between humanity and nature. In addition, a critical recognition of the importance and validity of inner consciousness and its mythic themes has been recognized as a key component for our survival. Indeed, we are on the threshold of a "new age," a new expression of the evolution of creation. As Arthur Clark said in the story "Star Child," written in 2010, "Something wonderful is going to happen!"[1]

So, we must ask ourselves, "What is our part in this great unfoldment, this re-birthing?" In short, "Why are we here?"

In this book we are going to explore the mythic journey known as the Quest. This journey is the "Royal Road of Initiation" which leads the spiritual aspirant from the role of spectator to that of co-creator. This is a journey within – deep within. It is a journey that is mirrored in all of the classic myths throughout all ages and civilizations. This theme can be found in the Bhagavad Gita, the

---

[1] Arthur C. Clarke, *2010: Odyssey Two*, 1982

Divine Comedy, Don Quixote and in the Bible. It is the story of the journey of the soul. And it is the story that we recognize in our daily lives once we have undertaken the Great Work of Transformation.

Forward

The forces and currents of the Hidden Light mold and shape our existence. But it is "The Ruler" within the Palace of our Hearts that controls and directs the currents of its creation. Thus, while our personality feels itself to be the subject of eternal, unceasing tides – it is mistaken. It is what we will call the Individuality that is of "royal" descent. If we could but look within ourselves and see our clear image in the pool of consciousness, we would see that reflection wears a royal diadem.

We must repeatedly remember to affirm our birthright and to do so by continual acts of attention. This is essential in these times of ordeal! For God has set certain obstacles, tests along our way, so that we try our skills and develop our strength in overcoming them. But for the trials there would be no triumph!

Table of Contents

Introductory Essays

Poke Runyon	ix
Tim Hogan	xi

Part One: The Way of the Mystic Warrior, An Introduction

The Quest	1
The Mystic Warrior	3
Know Thyself!	7
The Unfinished Creation	13
The Circle of Power	21
The Creative Power of Consciousness	27
The Gnostics	36
Where is God?	39

Part Two: The Way of Initiation, General Considerations

The Mystery of the Kingdom	49
The Three Stages	55
What is Initiation?	65
The Greater Initiation	74
The Lesser Mysteries	78
The Yoga of the West	89
The Master Pattern	98

The Ladder of Lights	107
Patterns on the Tree	121
Except The Lord Build the House	136
The Three Paths to Awakening	141

Part Three: The Method of the Mysteries

Within The Portal	147
The Initiation of Earth	150
The All is Mind	156
Consciousness Creates	167
The Principle of Attention	176
The Initiation of Air	183
How Consciousness Creates	189

Part Four: Archetypes

The Fertile Garden of Consciousness	197
If You Don't Go Within – You'll Go Without!	203
The Sense of Symbols	207
The Magical Library	219
The Initiation of Water	238
The Symbol in Action	241
The Power of Patterns	246
Ritual Magic and Ceremonial	252
Constructing the Form	260
Meditation: The Foundation of the Temple	270
Patanjali's Flow	280
The Power of Symbol in Ritual	283
The Four Maxims	291

The Initiation of Fire	306
You've Got to Have Heart!	310
To Purify, to Consecrate, to Make Holy	314
The Full Armor	324
The Child of Earth -- A Poem	345
The Dweller on the Threshold	346
The Three Tests of the Adept	356
The Greater Mysteries	375

Appendices

The Tower of Light Ritual	384
Commentary on the Ritual	404
Declaratio Lucis	409
Pathworkings	413

An Introduction, by Carroll "Poke" Runyon

(Author of *Secrets of the Golden Dawn Cypher Manuscript* and *The Book of Solomon's Magic.*)

I first met Paul Clark at a meeting of magicians in the home of my Golden Dawn mentor, the late Davis G. Kennedy, in 1982. Kennedy was one of a select group of students trained by Francis Israel Regardie (1907 – 1985). Although I had known Regardie rather well, I had been too much of a magical maverick to qualify as one of his students. Paul Clark came to the Golden Dawn tradition via *The Builders of the Adytum* (B.O.T.A.), founded by Paul Foster Case (1884 - 1954) and perpetuated by the late Ann Davies (1912 – 1975). Paul had been involved with the B.O.T.A. for many years and was deeply concerned over its direction since the passing of his mentor, the charismatic and inspiring Ms. Davies. Apparently Paul's concern was shared by Davies' successors: William Chesterman and Eugene Emard. In the year previous to our meeting in Kennedy's home, they had privately authorized Paul Clark to take whatever action he saw fit to preserve the "Inner Traditions" following their passing. To this end they had provided him with a complete corpus of the Paul Case initiatory system.

Our meeting at Kennedy's was significant. We were all determined to preserve the Western Esoteric Initiatory Tradition reconstituted in 1887 by the founders of The Golden Dawn. To this end we exchanged certain "secret" documents and pledged ourselves to mutual support. Even though Paul Clark's *Fraternity of the Hidden Light* is not "orthodox" Golden Dawn, and my *Order of the Temple of Astarte* is even more unorthodox, we have kept to that pledge.

Davis G. Kennedy and I established the *Isis-Osiris Temple* (Provisional) on the original Golden Dawn model in Pasadena, California (see *Secrets of the Golden Dawn Cypher Manuscript*). A year after Kennedy's death in 1985, we decided to close *Isis-Osiris* and support another of Regardie's students who had founded a regular G.D. temple in Glendale, California.

Meanwhile, Paul Clark, using Paul Foster Case's modified Golden Dawn and attracting the considerable worldwide audience that had been drawn to the writings of Case and Davies, was steadily and carefully building a stronger, better organized, and more highly populated "adytum" than anything Francis Regardie's legacy had - or has yet - been able to accomplish. The F.L.O., *Fraternitas L.V.X. Occulta* or Fraternity of the Hidden Light, now has sixteen groups worldwide with two more scheduled to be consecrated this next year. Why has this modified Golden Dawn been more successful in revival than its venerable grandparent? We can site the previous accomplishments of Case and Davies upon which the F.L.O. system is built along with the modest, unselfish dedication and positive leadership qualities of its "Steward" Dr. Paul Clark, but there may be another hidden or esoteric reason.

If I were the kind of egotistical magician the original Golden Dawn had a tendency to produce, I would disparage Case's replacement of the Golden Dawn's Enochian Tablets with a Hebrew configuration. We rough-and-ready magi take our Enochian straight up! And yet, even though I have spent years working and teaching the Enochian system (it was deeply embedded in the original Golden Dawn corpus and is a discrete sub-system in my own O.T.A.), I know its shortcomings and its dangers. I cannot seriously fault Paul Case, who was one of America's great magical adepts, for replacing it with tablets in Hebrew derived from the Qabalistic Cube of Space. Let me honestly admit that Dr. Dee's skryer, Edward Kelly, did not have a command of Greek, Hebrew or Latin. He could not channel one of those languages and thus he may have been subconsciously forced to create one using that innate "grammar machine" Noam Chomsky claims we are all born with. Certainly Enochian works. If I say *"Zacar od zamran,"* somewhere deep in your mind it rings a bell, but because it's Kelly's special language it might be the sound of a *cracked* bell. True or not, spiritually minded critics of the original Golden Dawn have blamed Enochian for stirring up the discordant magical currents that plagued the original Order.

In any case (pun intended), I contend that there was a lost Classical Master Mandala of the Universe, based on the Gnostic aeons concept, of which the Enochian Watchtowers are a later reflection (do not confuse this concept with the Tarot). Until this, "The Lost Word," is recovered, we need an acceptable substitute and Paul Foster Case may have provided one.

In further defense of Paul Foster Case on the Enochian issue we should remember that he was the first of the Western Adepti to fully embrace and employ the psycho-philosophy of Carl Jung, especially the theory of archetypes in the "Collective Unconsciousness." In Enochian, those archetypes are veiled and thus, to quote Regardie himself, they can be "capricious."

This Jungian archetype theory was a perfect complement to Paul Foster Case's major occult interest: the Tarot. Perhaps this emphasis on the Tarot trumps - which are attributed to the Paths rather than the Spheres of the Tree of Life - was responsible for Case's Western version of the Indian Chakras. Personally, I am an advocate of the Hermetic "Lightning Flash" or the Sephiroth = Chakras configuration, but I will still concede that Case's Paths = Chakras configuration may have merit as an internal alchemical meditation. In this instance, Case followed the lead of the great French mage Eliphas Levi who held that the Tarot was much older than now supposed, and that it was the secret key to the Qabalah. Levi's Tarot-to-Path attributions had a profound influence on the Golden Dawn, and subsequently on Case and Davies. Regardless of how much or how little emphasis one wishes to place on the Tarot, we must concede that it has become an integral part of the modern Hermetic Qabalah. (Readers aware of the recent revival of Hebrew "Kabbalah," without Tarot cards or other

Hermetic infusions, should realize that Kabbalah - notwithstanding its Assyrian, Pythagorean and Gnostic roots - strives to be exclusively Jewish.)

In this book Dr. Paul Clark deals at length and in depth with those very important aspects of the Western Tradition which he and his sponsors were determined to preserve: *the purpose, the process and the promise of initiation.* He rightly insists that the initiate must "do the Work" and that there is no magical "free lunch." While conceding the power of the magical tradition, or *egregore,* he firmly insists that the student must make the traditional *Names and Images* his own in order for them to effect a genuine transformation. He manages to describe this subtle and complex process in simple, straightforward language that any reasonably intelligent person can understand. This in itself is a remarkable accomplishment and a valuable contribution.

Clark keeps to a high spiritual, ethical and moral tone throughout. He makes it clear that the ultimate goal of the Western Esoteric tradition is personal enlightenment and service to humankind. There is no offer of mysterious supernatural powers, but *The Great Secret of All Powers* and *The Holy Grail* itself is clearly and beautifully explained. It is also revealed that the unfolding process of spiritual development through initiation should lead the initiate to fully understand and incorporate this Great Secret in his mind and heart. Paul Clark firmly states that all work in the Western Tradition should lead to this goal.

However, let us not make the mistake of thinking

that Clark's high moral tone connotes a narrow, puritanical approach to life or to magick. What we have here is the true philosophy of the adept who is kind to others because he knows that the God inside them is the same as the God within himself. He controls his passions not because he is afraid of punishment or criticism, but because he channels these natural urges into attaining a higher state of consciousness, which he can then inspire others to attain.

In keeping with this philosophy, Paul Clark modestly assumes the title of "Steward" of the Fraternity of the Hidden Light. We might say that within the pages of this book he has revealed that "Hidden Light," but Paul would tell you, and I would agree, that no matter what intellectual understanding you may have of "The Great Work," you must actually do it in order for the Light to truly shine forth from within.

Poke Runyon,
At Rivendell Hermitage, California

An Introduction, by Timothy Hogan

(Author of *The Way of the Templar*, *Entering the Chain of Union*, and *The Alchemical Keys to Masonic Ritual*)

The jungle of Western esotericism can be hard to venture through. There are places that are wild and even unruly, and other places that are beautiful and serene. One thing is certain: it is a jungle in which there are so many different types of vegetation, from so many places, each of which have been planted and allowed to grow in its own way over many years. Wading through it all and trying to make sense of it can be daunting and even forbidding for any traveler on the quest. Simply cataloguing it all can take a lifetime of research. And then, there is the next phase of trying to make sense of it and finding the proper use of it all. Many people get lost in the jungle, unable to synthesize and integrate it into their way of understanding. However, every once in a while, there is the rare guide; one who has been able, not only to catalogue it, but to develop a working science that can distill its essence into a formula for rejuvenation. This formula can, in turn, enliven all those who venture into the territory. Dr. Paul Clark is one of these rare individuals, who has not only come to learn the territory, but has developed a method to transform it and utilize it. He has applied the principles of the

Great Work.

In being able to study an advanced copy of this book, it immediately became apparent that Dr. Clark had been able to interpret the subject matter and express it in a form suitable for practical application. This has been the hope of all mystery traditions, of all times. Drawing from the wisdom of the great Adepti who have left their mark in ages past, Dr. Clark has managed to interpret and clarify much of what they had to say. Consequently, the careful reader will discover in the following pages some of the great secrets related to the purpose of initiation, of Qabalistic correspondence, of Hermetic perspective, of the secret messages of tarot, as well as fundamental keys that are critical for understanding the reason for ritual movements that spring from strands like the Rosicrucian and Masonic traditions. It is no secret that as the custodian of the important writings and teachings of Paul Foster Case, which were deposited within the Fraternity of Hidden Light, Dr. Paul Clark is infinitely suited to be a spokesperson for the tradition he represents. However, what he presents can be a useful map for people of all traditions, as contained within these pages are the philosophical keys for the truly universal Source for such manifestations.

On a personal note, I have spent years traveling to many far reaches of the globe and considerable time meeting with the leadership of different spiritual currents, all in the hope of finding "new keys" that can unlock many of the enigmas of the Western Esoteric Tradition. Imagine my delight and surprise while reading this book, to find many of the secrets at my fingertips! Dr. Clark has outlined much of the work, thereby saving any spiritual seeker many years of personal research.

The important work before you is not one to be read quickly and without intention. Rather, it is one that will require concentration and introspection of you, and finally integration. Dr. Clark has outlined it as a working manual for the practitioner of any western discipline. In fact, he has done most of the work for you, by synthesizing it into an effective model. This is what makes this book unique, different from many of the intellectual and in some ways impractical tracts of the Western Esoteric Tradition.

May it be for you a lamp, which will unveil the dark corners and unknown territories of the jungle that has grown (and maybe even become overgrown), over the centuries. I can say with certainty that a serious digestion of this material will bring you one step closer to the Mastery that you seek. Therefore, read on with intention!

In the Bonds of Spiritual Chivalry,

Timothy W. Hogan
Chevalier Emerys

PART ONE

The Voyage of the Mystic Warrior, An Introduction

Chapter 1
The Quest

Quantum Physics asserts that everything in the Universe is energy – energy in motion! Metaphysics has always stated that everything is consciousness.

> *"The All is mind, the Universe is mental."*
> *– The Kybalion, p. 26*

Initiates affirm that the point of creation is within. More and more rapidly we see these viewpoints coincide, validating each other. It is interesting to note that modern philosophies, such as "New Thought," are confirming what Ageless Wisdom has always taught.

These doctrines were once the province of the Mystery schools, available only to a carefully tested, select few and guarded by initiatic oaths. Today, we can harness these techniques to help us realize our full potential and achieve our destiny of enlightenment. Properly used, these ancient disciplines and skills can help us to realize health, happiness and love.

In this book we will explore the ultimate goal of the Mystery teachings. We will discuss how consciousness works and how the Divine energy manifests differently at the several levels of the creative process. We will compare the Qabalistic and Hermetic systems to modern sacred psychology. We will learn how to access the "Council Chamber of the Masters" and to receive the advice of our inner teacher.

Chapter 2
The Mystic Warrior

I have always been fascinated by the martial arts. I especially love the traditional arts based upon Zen or Taoist philosophy. I have found them to be among many paths to self-knowledge. Such has been my fascination, that I have devoted over two decades to pursuing (and finally achieving) a Black Belt.

Early on in this process, I might have thought that the achievement of a Black Belt represented the end of the voyage. If so, I was mistaken --- it was only the beginning! It is only <u>after</u> earning this rank that the practitioner is in a position to understand what the art form is really about. Only after having achieved this goal, have I been able to concentrate less on the mechanics of the techniques and more upon the philosophy at its basis – "The Tao."

Initiation is also like this. Only after spending many years engrossed within the teachings and practices of a genuine initiatory school, after we think "we have arrived," do we find the reality, the process, the "Way!"

I remember, once, back in the early days of the Fraternity of the Hidden Light, when one of our members, who was working through some psychological projections, made a comment to another initiate that eventually found its way back to me. He wondered, he said, if the Group Mind was being influenced by my involvement in the martial arts and causing some of his own anger issues! He didn't feel that it was proper for a spiritual teacher to be involved in what he interpreted as a discipline concerned with fighting.

I reflected on his comment. I realized that he was rejecting his own responsibility for his behavioral patterns; but was I contributing to his tests?

After careful meditation, I concluded that he was in error. A teacher <u>may</u> indeed have a significant effect upon his students. However, this member had revealed that he lacked a real understanding of what I have chosen to call "the Voyage of the Mystic Warrior." This is a misunderstanding of what a Warrior really is.

It is surprising how many aspirants lack balance in their ideas about what constitutes a true spiritual attitude. Influenced by movies and pseudo-mystics, they elevate pacifism and etherialism, at the expense of justice and practicality. Some feel that any martial and assertive tendency is bad; indeed, that any expression of the physical universe is inherently unspiritual. However, the way of the initiate is actually the pursuit of a greater balance. Thus Hermes, the great predynastic Egyptian sage, tells us "Equilibrium is the secret of the Great Work."

Additionally, my student confused the characteristics of a true "Warrior with those of a mere fighter. The fighter responds to confrontation presented from without by an opponent. He must win at any cost or his self-assessed worth and his prestige, defined by others, is lessened. "My cause, right or wrong!" is his motto. The "Warrior, on the other hand, has dedicated his life to an inner code of conduct. He faces both success and failure with poise and equanimity, always seeking an inner point of stability. The Warrior places himself in the flow and becomes one with the "Dance of Life." And, perhaps most importantly, the Warrior realizes that he is on a voyage or journey. This is a voyage of Self-discovery, a journey to completeness, a mystic voyage of awakening, of illumination. Every true initiate is a "Warrior of the Spirit."

Although this voyage is unique to each sojourner, there are some characteristics, some landmarks that we may share, making it possible to help each other along the Path. This is the purpose of this book. But reading the roadmap is not a substitute for taking the trip. We must set our course and go forth. Also we must remember to enjoy the scenery and the company of the fellow pilgrims we may encounter along the way. Remember, as Lao Tzu said, the Journey of 10,000 miles begins with the first step. "Bon Voyage!"

Chapter 3
Know Thyself!

"Know Thyself!" These were the words carved over the doorway of the Temple of Apollo at Delphi. It seems, at first glance, a simple exhortation to self-analysis. But, after due meditation, much more is revealed.

In looking for the roots of the mystical, initiatic tradition, we are led to the Halls of Khem (Egypt), and to the courts of Solomon's Temple. Here, we may find the symbols that lead our consciousness toward the techniques and disciplines of Self-knowledge. Here, we find the ageless symbols of Water and Fire.

Water, both as a symbol of purification and consciousness, emphasizes the necessity of diligently purging all error to the extent possible from our habitual thinking patterns. This is especially true when we use expressions that begin with the words "I AM."

Complementary to this is the practice connected with the element of Fire, the symbol of the Divine Spirit. This element is used to consecrate, that is to "make holy," to align with that spirit.

The Hebrew word for knowledge or "to know" is *Da'ath*. It is also the name attributed to the mystical quasi-sephirah of the Tree of Life that divides the world of Divinity from the world of Mind. It therefore stands in the midst of "The Abyss." (We will discuss the Tree in more detail in the next section.) This attribution to a station on the Tree has always been a puzzle to students of the Qabalah. Why is mere "knowledge," they often ask, held to be more "spiritual" and closer to the Source of All than concepts such as "Beauty" or "Mercy", for example? The key to this apparent contradiction is suggested by the fact that Da'ath, stands halfway up along the Path of Gimel, the 13th Path attributed to the Uniting Intelligence. This reminds us of the older, Biblical meaning of the verb "to know." Here it refers to "Union." On the physical plane, this refers to sexual union, but it also suggests union on all other levels of expression. Thus, for our purposes, Da'ath refers to the knowledge gained from "Union." This knowledge is referred to as "Gnosis" or "Mystery." It is this objective that impels the initiates of the esoteric mystical tradition of the west. Therefore the injunction to "Know Thyself," is an admonishment to become one with the True Self residing at the center of our consciousness – our Higher Self – the Individuality!

The Alchemists have a saying that "Nature unaided always fails." I remember, as a young speaker, once quoting this to an audience. One of the listeners, (an older fellow, probable upset with a 20-year old kid being the featured speaker at the event) vehemently challenged me, asking how I could possibly presume to criticize nature and God in His workings. I answered by asking him for what purpose he supposed that creation was ordained? He pressed me to tell him! I, instead, asked another question: Did he think that humankind, as it is now constituted, represented the pinnacle of God's achievement? He answered, "No." I agreed and then continued, indicating that humankind had only made it thus far by natural evolution – that is, by nature. But, if we were to stop at this point, the whole experiment would be an abysmal failure! God's purpose is far grander and more sublime. It is nothing less than the perfect reflection of His Wisdom, Power and Love. But to achieve this destiny, we must enter into a partnership with Nature. It was Her purpose to get us to this stage, but it required the power of the Divine, functioning through an illuminated self-consciousness to complete the journey. This is our job, to become conscious co-creators. This is our work – The Great Work!

We humans are the expression of God's desire for the embodiment of perfect knowledge and unconditional love functioning through a will that is free. And since God is all knowing and all loving, the goal of that desire is already fulfilled in our hearts and souls.

When we look upon our brothers and sisters and focus on that which separates and makes us different, we are focusing upon our fear that we are "not-enough;" that we are less than God knows we are.

To look at another, even though that person appears to be full of hate, full of fear, full of disease; that person is an expression of the Divine. These appearances and these preconceived imperfections are calls of a soul for help. They are calls of a soul in search of the love of God. This is the one love that is identical with the light they bear within. Although it is shaded and we may not see it, if we look for it with pure intention, we shall find it and finding it, we may fan it with the breath of our compassion into the star that it really is.

The human touch is a miracle. It can rescue a person from despair. It can heal depression and restore an individual's sense of self-worth. It can affirm the truth of our Oneness and refute the lie of separation.

Consider the great cathedrals, temples and churches that humans have raised to God. Who has not gazed at the sunlight shining through the beautiful gothic rose window of Notre Dame de Paris and not felt the thrill of a sacred moment? Some may have had the opportunity to worship in the Crystal Cathedral and, looking up, saw an airplane soaring majestically in the sky above. Yes, many and great are the edifices raised by human piety to uplift the spirit and pay homage to their creator. But, greater still are the cathedrals and temples raised by God for humanity. The awe-inspiring beauty of majestic trees lifting their branches to heaven and at the same time lifting our spirits. Great mountains, beaches, and canyons, where God's choir of gull, eagle and songbird sing their eternal adorations. Which of us has not felt our souls soar as we gaze at the immenseness of the star-sprinkled night. Yet, even these are not our greatest temples. For the greatest, most sacred temples are to be found in the sanctuary of the loving human spirit. Oh seeker, know thy Self!

Chapter 4
The Unfinished Creation

He wore a long robe and carried a staff, his full sleeves flapping as he moved around the elaborately drawn circle upon the floor through clouds of incense. He would point his staff at a design on the floor and would raise his voice in a vibrant chant, urgently calling forth from the deep those powers at which we could only guess!

I sat mesmerized, as the magician depicted on the television continued his performance. I was watching the television program called "Thriller!" and the episode was "The Dark Legacy," and I was twelve years old.

All of a sudden, I said with conviction to my mother: "He's doing it all wrong! He should be standing inside the circle, not outside!" My mother looked at me in surprise, and asked: "And just how would you know that?"

Suddenly, realizing what I had said and judging her reaction by the look on her face, I fell back on that time-honored response all kids give their folks and said, "Huh?"

But what I suddenly had realized is that I remembered wearing robes and carrying a staff. I remembered performing a ceremony similar to the one I was watching on the Tube. Thus, I had my first encounter with what I was later to learn was called a past life recovery and reincarnation. Reincarnation is a belief held by at least a quarter of the world's populace. Reincarnation is an important component in Paganism and is also found in the belief systems of Buddhism, Hinduism, Taoism, Judaism as well as early Christianity. Therefore, the idea that we have lived other lives before is not as exotic or strange as our friendly neighborhood minister or priest would perhaps have us believe.

But why? Why would we choose, or be required, to come back repeatedly to face the same temptations and challenges, life after life? Because we are an unfinished creation! While most educated people today generally accept the notion of the physical evolution of species, two aspects of this process are relatively esoteric.

A corresponding evolution of consciousness is not well known. The mental potential of humanity remains largely untapped. There are little known powers and skills that are, as yet, undeveloped in the vast majority of individuals. Exoteric scientists will admit that the average adult utilizes only approximately 10 percent of his brain! They can only guess what potential remains in the unknown 90 percent. This potential is being developed slowly by Nature. In some cases, it is accelerated by deliberate, mystical disciplines.

The other fact that is often overlooked is that physical evolution is ongoing as well, not only through random, natural selection, but also by another method. This is the path of the initiate, of mystical transfiguration, the transmutation from "natural humanity to the illuminated vehicle of the adept!"

In the late 1960's, what had been known by mystics, shamans and occultists for centuries was brought to the attention of the general public. "acid," "magic mushrooms," "pot," etc., introduced the world to the idea that the alteration of blood chemistry can affect perceived reality. However, what is still relatively unknown outside of the esoteric disciplines, is the fact that consciousness itself, may be capable of altering blood chemistry. One of the active ingredients in LSD is serotonin, which acts upon the central nervous system. Coincidently, during the greater initiatory process of illumination, as the serpent fire is raised along the central spinal column and enters the pineal center, it fuses what is known as "brain sand" into a crystalline structure. Analysis of this material reveals it to be comprised of --serotonin! Therefore, adepts who have access to and control of advanced states of consciousness are, in fact, physically of an advanced evolutionary form!

This should not be interpreted as an elitist statement, for this is the destiny of all, whether reached by the long, gradual path of natural evolution or the short, intensely challenging path of initiation.

Thus, in our present state we are unfinished creations. This is, as I have pointed out, implied in the saying of the Hermetic sages, "Nature unaided always fails." Nature requires an accomplice and that partner is the human consciousness awakening to the possibility of illuminated transformation. For this purpose of self/Divine perfection, we enter into the "School of Life," again and again until we graduate and, perhaps, return as instructors.

In the traditions associated with Freemasonry, we hear the story of the building of King Solomon's temple. Great detail is provided as to the various features of the building. We are told about the different floors, the pillars, the various altars, secret chambers, stairways, etc. All of these details are symbolic. They provide an allegorical scenario to depict the perfection of human consciousness and the completion of physical transformation.

The narration stipulates that when the Temple was completed, the presence of God, known as the Shekinah, descended and dwelt in the Holy of Holies. This presence was so overwhelming that it drove the priests from the sanctum. Priests are intermediaries, so it can be inferred that when our adytum is completed, all barriers, all need for intermediaries is at an end. We then become one with God and see the glory of the Divine face to face.

We see the implication of this idea in the Christian Gospels, where Jesus is transformed on the Mountain of Transfiguration. Another example is more modern. We have only to look at the reverse of the Great Seal of the United States to see evidence of this concept that "a work in progress" was accepted by the Founding Fathers of the United States, many of whom were initiates. Here, we see an unfinished pyramid, a temple, being completed by the hand of Providence, placing a glorious triangular capstone on its pinnacle. This "All-seeing Eye" represents the divine conscious intervention, sometimes called "Grace," that completes the work. Here, we may, once again, remember the Holy Scriptures, where it is written: "Except the Lord builds the House, they labor in vain who build it." (*Psalms* 127:1)

This theme of a transformational journey or voyage is repeated time and time again in holy writings. In the Garden of Eden story, we see humankind dwelling in a state of innocent bliss, an unconscious oneness. Then, at the urging of the serpent of wisdom, called the Tempter, we eat of the fruit of the Tree of Knowledge. We become aware of "good and evil," and all other opposites! We become aware of the consciousness of separation, of individualism. It is interesting to note that, according to the Qabalists' system of interpretation known as *gematria*, the word for serpent, *nachash* and the word for messiah, *messiach*, both equal 358, by numeration. This implies a close relationship, usually an underlying identification.

According to the "Fall-up," theory, the story of humanity's expulsion from the Garden of Eden represents mankind's evolution from unconscious to self-conscious stages of evolution. The Bible furnishes us with many additional stories of transformation from the stage of conscious separation to one of conscious oneness, also termed "Cosmic Consciousness." Whenever, in scripture, we see characters taking journeys or having their names changed, we may wish to look closer. Many times we will see that this corresponds to an "awakening" or a "completion" experience. For example, Abram became Abraham, Jacob became Israel, and Saul became Paul.

As the first book of the Christian Codex or Cannon narrates the beginning of our journey, it is interesting that the last book of this collection provides one of the best examples of the completion of the process. In the book of *Revelation* we read about the descent of the "Heavenly Jerusalem." This symbolizes the awakened state of adepthood. This journey or voyage represents a quest for completion and realization of the embodiment of our destined potential.

Chapter 5
The Circle of Power

Esoteric or spiritual science differs from exoteric or materialistic science in the belief and knowledge of inner worlds. However, many schools of psychology (notably Jungian) also posit these inner states. (Of course, psychology isn't really considered a science by hard scientists, such as physicists!)

These inner worlds of consciousness are accessed through our personal subconscious minds. Symbolically, this may be thought of as if each of us were an inlet or bay through which we are able to reach a great ocean. Although our bay of subconsciousness seems to be distinct, there is no real separation.

It is this inner world that is the source of all creative processes, not just of great inspirations and works of art, but literally every creative process, ranging from our smallest acts of problem solving to the creation of the entire manifest universe.

Our personal subconsciousness controls most of our bodily functions. I would be willing to bet that no one who reads these words is keeping their heart beating or digesting their food through the strength of their intellect. These functions, together with innumerable others, are performed beneath the threshold of awareness, our conscious waking minds. Additionally, it is the subconscious mind that builds the connections and opens the opportunities that assist us to reach our goals and realize our dreams. Why, we may ask, does subconsciousness appear to give us what we want only some of the time? Why do we achieve our goals and fulfill our vision, our dreams, only sometimes? Why do some "lucky" people reached their goal while others seem destined to share only the crumbs that happen to fall from the table of fulfillment?

George Bernard Shaw once wrote a play called *Pygmalion,* about a cockney flower girl named Eliza Doolittle who became the subject of a wager between a man named Henry Higgins and one of his associates. The bet depended on whether Mr. Higgins could pass Ms. Doolittle off as a sophisticated, highborn socialite at an upper-crust social event. You will, of course, recognize that this play became the famous Broadway musical, *My Fair Lady*. Higgins found that no amount of coaching or bullying was successful until Eliza actually accepted the possibility that she <u>could</u> be transformed into the debutante. It was a question of self-image. Was she able to picture herself this way? Hence, this phenomenon has become known as the "Pygmalion effect." This mechanism, popularly referred to as the "self-fulfilling prophecy," is of central importance to our successful navigation of life and our own ability to achieve our goals.

Why? Because all of creation proceeds from these inner worlds of consciousness. Never, in the outside world of manifestation, will we ever find anything that causes us to think, feel, do or be anything! Causation is within. We choose how to react to the events, conditions and appearances that are presented to us by the world of manifestation. We create our personal universe and decide how we experience reality on a moment-to-moment basis, based upon the images we habitually hold in our consciousness and choose to energize with our desire force. These energized images become the matrix of our manifestation. Every clear, emotionally charged, mental image will tend to manifest itself as an actual condition or event.

Thus, our self-image becomes our self-fulfilling prophecy. Our self-concept is perhaps the most important image that we hold. The picture we have of ourselves determines how we relate to each other, to the universe and to God. It determines how we react to the mirror of our environment; how we confront and adjust to the growth stimuli and challenges our Individuality (Higher Self) sets for us.

Our subconscious mind is completely amenable to the suggestions conveyed through imagery. If we hold images of poor self-worth, poor health, poverty and conflict, our "servant" willingly supplies the conditions and circumstances that fulfill these suggestions. That's the bad news. The good news is, that it will be just as cooperative in manifesting our positive images of health, love and abundance. We have a choice.

The difficulty is that most people are inconsistent. They have not fully realized this causal link. This very inconsistency supports the illusion of causality by external circumstances and, if reinforced by corresponding images, results in still more self-fulfilling prophecies.

One who is awakened to this law must confront the big "R" word – RESPONSIBILITY. Never can he defend actions by relying on "thus and so caused me to do…" or "they make me so…" or "it isn't my fault", or even "The Devil made me do it!" He realizes that he is responsible for the creative images that populate his world.

The up side of this equation is that the awakened one realizes that if he is responsible, that he is in control. He controls through his images. And if these images reflect archetypal potencies, he can transform his entire being and achieve the full potential of his destiny. He stands within the circle of his power and remains one with his true Self.

Chapter 6
The Creative Power of Consciousness

It is a demonstrable, observable fact that every act of creation begins with an act of mind. Paul Case wrote that every clear mental image will tend to materialize itself as an actual condition or event. Hermes declared that, "The Universe is mental!" What do these statements mean? What implications do they have, not only for the initiate, but for every one of us?

As we have previously explained, causality is internal. It is a function of consciousness. We continually function as co-creators with the Divine. Our universe is shaped by the mental images we habitually choose to hold and energize with our emotional power. The multiverse is a closed system, moving according to universal law. There is no chaos. There is no chance. However, since Cosmos creates in accordance with our images, if we choose to model our reality based upon the concepts of materialism, mortality and separation, our personal world becomes a manifestation of these lies. This is the reason that an individual can point to examples where appearances seem to support their thesis of randomness, etc. They are simply self-fulfilling prophecies. The truth is otherwise. As Einstein put it, "God does not play dice with the Universe!"

The Hermeticists conceive of the Cosmos as being a vast mental "image" held in the Universal Mind. This is also affirmed by many of the major schools of the Eastern Tradition. Further, it is affirmed that there is no separation between manifestation of the "Inner" and the "Outer." Both are part of the same continuum.

This continuum is explained in the Qabalah as the four "Olahms" or Worlds. These explain the flow of the creative energy from the Divine, from pure will to the manifest and back again. This should be regarded as a functional model only; it does not suggest that there is any place where God is not nor is there any aspect of the universe that is less sacred than any other. Rather, the Worlds of the Qabalists can be conceived of as four different stages or modes in the creative process, moving from abstract to finite manifestation.

The World of Assiah

Starting with the manifest and working our way "up" or "within" we find Assiah. This is the world of the manifest. It is characterized by apparent separation. It is the area of appearances, conditions and events. Here we see the One Energy expressing through form. Everywhere we look in the manifest world we observe this rule. Even color and sound, two very powerful tools for attuning to inner forces, are manifestations of form.

Form should not be interpreted as inert or dead. The very concept that something is either alive or dead is a superficial one. All physical manifestations, in whatever forms they occur, are expressions of the One Living Consciousness. In Assiah, in the parlance of the "Practical Qabalah," we find the beings known as "the Elementals."

The term Elementals refers to that same "consciousness" that is behind molecular and atomic levels of the finite world. This also includes what is known as the "etheric" level. This electro-magnetic, subtle aspect of the physical is the basis of "ectoplasm," that which plays an important part in the séance room phenomena of Spiritualism. This level is of importance also in the esoteric work of healing and the so-called "invisible" work of a lodge of the Western Mysteries. These etheric levels act as a "matrix" upon which the physical world is patterned.

Dr. Jean Houston (1987) coined a phrase in her writing that aptly expresses the thought processes exhibited at the level of Assiah. She called it "this is Me," which refers to the focus on distinctness, uniqueness, and separation on this plane.

The World of Yetzirah

Yetzirah, or the "World of Formation" corresponds to the "Astral Plane" of the Theosophists and the "Collective Unconscious" of the Jungian psychoanalytic school. At this level we are all connected. Here, we share the great thoughts and inspirations of Jesus, Moses, Buddha, etc. In the same way, we are also linked to the consciousnesses of a Hitler or Genghis Kahn! Moreover, we find relationships with the group consciousness of all other species. Thus, the characteristic thought processes that describes this level would be perhaps, equivalent to Dr. Houston's "This is We!"

Here, the Divine energy expresses through symbols and images. On the plane of Assiah, relationships are measured by duration, or the standard speed necessary to move from one location to another. In Yetzirah, however, proximity is measured by relationships in consciousness, how one concept is symbolically associated with another. We've all experienced dreams where we move from one scenario to another simply by "thinking it."

In pathworkings and other vision work, it is common to become sidetracked or to move to another symbolic environment, just by allowing the mind to wander. This work is so seriously considered among the esoteric orders, that a series of testing techniques has been developed to assist initiates by allowing them to "test the spirits" that they may encounter.

In Qabalah, Malkuth carries the attribution "Cholem Yesodoth." This is a personified symbol whose name may be translated as "Breaker of the Foundations." It refers to the fact that there is a certain "inertia" or "memory" that retards or purifies the imagery matrix before it is allowed to enter into expression or manifest as conditions or events. This is important, for, as it has been observed by the wise, if all of our mental images became manifest, we would have ceased to exist ages ago. Interestingly enough, this was the premise of the now classic science fiction movie *Forbidden Planet.* In this film, the "Krell" an advanced race whose home planet was "Altare IV," had developed an external technology that enabled them to manifest their mental creations instantly. However, they had forgotten that this device, although connected to their conscious minds, also responded to unconscious suggestions on the levels of the "Id." These levels accessed dark and primitive urges. Thus, while they slept, the machines manifested the nightmares that originated in savage areas of the unconscious minds so that the Krell were ultimately annihilated!

Yetzirah acts as the "matrix" for manifestation. In order to alter physical reality, we must first alter this matrix. Causation is within. Every adept must first recognize, and proceed to redeem their "Shadow." We, as individual aspirants, therefore seek to transmute our unregenerated patterns of consciousness that would otherwise function as "original sin."

The World of Briah

In the World of Creation or "Briatic World" we encounter the forces of the Divine called *archetypal.* These have been personified as the "Archangels." The reader should be careful to note the difference between the "archetypal images," found in Yetzirah and the archetypes themselves, found in Briah. These archetypes access the conscious potencies that function in Briah. Contacting these potencies is an altogether different matter than working with their symbolic counterparts in the World of Formation!

Our Most Greatly Honored Soror Resurgam, (Ann Davies), always taught us to contact these higher forces through their corresponding images and symbols, for example, as they are represented in the Tarot. These act as circuit breakers do, in case any personal imbalances in the constitution of the operator cause problems when such contacts are established. Without this protection, direct connections with these potencies themselves might actually shatter the vehicles of the aspirant. This can be compared to the relative safety of contacting an electrical current when it is properly grounded as opposed to being struck by lightning when the unfortunate target serves as the ground! This is referred to in mystical literature as "walking with God and is not."

The Archangels provide a measure of protection. In this regard, since the Divine energy is manifested at this level as consciousness, and, providing the motivation of the operator is correct, the Archangels act as benevolent mediators.

In the world of Briah, mentation functions as "I Am" consciousness. Distinctions exist in regard to identity, but identity is synonymous with the primary creative power. No longer are we the lens or the colored glass that modifies the manifestation of the light---we have become the light itself.

The World of Atziluth

In the primordial world of Atziluth, the Divine creative energy simply IS, without qualification or limitation. Here the realization of the "I Am" has transformed into the identification with the "I." The only I. Here, the limits, the boundaries of separation fade into the clear light of unity. More cannot be said!

So we see that every creative impulse begins at the level of the Divine and proceeds towards manifestation, stage by stage, first as the Divine impulse, then through the defining image, emotionally charged, to materialize itself as an actual condition or event.

Chapter 7
The Gnostics

The Gnostics were mystics who existed side by side with early Christians, until driven underground by the persecution of the Orthodoxy when it started to consolidate its political power at the time of the Nicene Council. Certain sects of the Gnostics held that an evil god known as the Demiurge had created the manifested universe. This was not the true God, but He who dwelt apart from the world of time and space, in the Empyrean world; this was the deity that ensnared humanity into the bondage of the material world. Therefore, the "mission" of the Gnostic aspirant was to escape from the illusion of the material universe by ascending through the "Seven Heavens" to enter into the real world of light and truth, governed by the divine *Sophia* (Wisdom). To do this, the spiritual seeker must pass through seven portals. At each portal, a guardian, known as an "Archon", would confront them. This entity would demand a password or mantra and a sign before the aspirant would be allowed to pass into the corresponding heaven.

The aspirant penetrates the veil of reality

I remember thinking, "What a fairy tale!" Yet, the Gnostics were not only among the most sophisticated and intellectually advanced thinkers of their era, they were also initiates. Therefore, I reasoned, there must be a deeper, more mystical explanation.

I contemplated the figure of the Demiurge. Was there an "evil god that creates our universe and ensnares us in matter? As a matter of fact, yes! Our own creative consciousness, when directed by our fear-filled, insecure, false-reasoning ego, is just such a creator! To awaken from this dream of separation and impotence will open the seven levels of awareness referred to, in some literature as the *chakras*, or inner centers. Techniques for accomplishing this often utilize meditative visualizations combined by intoning certain sacred vowel sounds. This is performed with the goal of achieving enlightenment, illumination, Cosmic Consciousness, Nirvana, etc. At this level of awareness we may become awakened instruments for God's creativity and witnesses of the divine power of consciousness.

Chapter 8
Where is God?

I have always been gifted with an extremely vivid imagination. But, I have also learned, from a very early age, to maintain the balance between "outer" and "inner" reality. Many focus on the, so-called, "real world," with its ever-shifting panoply of conditions, appearances and events. The inability or unwillingness to accept other levels of reality other than the physical leads to a myopia that places the individual outside the flow of the creative source. Chance becomes, for these persons, a major factor in their equation of life. Money and power becomes the "grail" of the Materialist.

At the other extreme, is the individual who lives all of his life in his head. Instead of experiencing life, this person fantasizes about it. This person may also analyze each situation to death, afraid to act. This has been referred to as, "The paralysis of analysis!" Such a person may be described as the classic introvert. We must utilize the manifest world as our barometer, carefully evaluating how our mental creations take form; in this way, the world becomes "our magic mirror."

As I have mentioned, it is a balancing act – one of maintaining appropriate "equilibrium." For the mystic, the separation temporarily disappears, and the Inner becomes one with the Outer.

When I was about nine years old, I awoke with anticipation and excitement! My Little League baseball team had had an outstanding season! And now, this very day, at 10 AM, we would be playing, for the "All City Championship" of Tulsa, Oklahoma. I eagerly dressed in my uniform and pushed my glove, cleats and favorite bat into my duffle bag. I put my jacket on for it was cool -- for the very good reason that it was six o'clock in the morning! Nobody else was up, so I decided to walk off my nervousness. I hiked the three quarters of a mile to my sister's house. Her next-door neighbor's son was also on my team. I figured we would play catch and "loosen up." As a nine year old, I couldn't imagine why they weren't up at dawn also - but, they weren't. So, I decided to walk another mile or so to the ballpark.

When I arrived at the field it was still early, and worse yet, it had begun to rain. "A little rain never hurt anyone!" I said to myself, unwilling to believe that my championship-destined game might be rained out. But, as the minutes ticked by, it began to rain harder and harder, until I was in the midst of a legendary, Oklahoma downpour.

As I now considered the distinct probability that the championship would have to wait for another (and drier) day, I started the long walk home in the rain. As I plodded along, now completely soaked, I slipped into a reverie. I didn't realize it at the time, but I had entered a deep state of meditation.

I had recently discovered in the school library books on Greek and Roman Mythology. I had become fascinated by the stories of adventures of the Heroes, Gods and Goddesses of Olympus. I had, even at that young age, came to the conclusion that these ancient people had personified the forces of nature as their Gods. However, as I walked in the downpour, I experienced a direct intuitive perception. It was the realization, that these phenomena of nature were not blind forces, but, in fact, ensouled, conscious aspects of the Divine! It was as if innumerable, invisible companions were accompanying me upon my walk. These intelligences existed in and through the natural phenomena expressing around me. I was part of their dance and they were acting as "guardians" of the young boy who was a guest in their world. The vital force flowing through me from these friends was tremendous, filling me with exhilaration verging on the ecstatic! I realize today, that I had touched the unseen world and had a glimpse of the consciousness that resides there.

Five years later this insight would again be presented to me, in a more "classical" form. I had been accepted, about a year earlier, for training in a modern day esoteric school founded by the Tarot expert, the late Dr. Paul

Foster Case. Because of my young age, this required the personal dispensation of Dr. Case's successor, Ann Davies. The daily regimen of study and meditation on the Tarot and Qabalah delighted me. Dr. Case's courses of instruction on these mystical subjects, in my opinion, are still among the very best available. I had not realized to what extent the studies and meditations had begun their process of slow transformation. That is, until one summer dawn of my fifteenth year.

I had decided to keep a vigil. At the time, I didn't know that this was what it was called. In the early evening, I had started to study and meditate on the seventh Key of the Tarot Major Arcana called "The Chariot." The ideas of receptivity and "letting go and letting God," associated with this symbol, were weaving a mystical pattern through my thoughts. Coincidently, I had just received a book as a gift. It was the theosophical classic, *Light on The Path*, by Mabel Collins.

In this book, I read about the quest for the "Warrior Within," that Mystic Warrior who is symbolic of our true Self or the Individuality.

This is that point of balance, of eternity, where our soul connects with the Infinite. The nexus of these different ideas fell like the particles of colored glass in a kaleidoscope, suddenly and without effort, into a beautiful and symmetrical pattern of realization. The "aha" of a direct knowing or illumination that there is deep within me and flowing through me, a greater consciousness than my personality. This "essence" expressed qualities of omnipresence, omnipotence, omniscience, and, perhaps most importantly, "omni-beneficence." With this awakening came the certainty of a purpose or destiny that would guide and illuminate this incarnation.

Still in ecstasy, I stepped from the front door of my parent's farmhouse and gazed eastward, across the fields and woods, toward the rapidly approaching dawn. I saw the sun rising above the trees.

As the sun's rays kissed the earth, I became aware that every leaf, every creature, every bird and every drop of dew, was infused with an immanent consciousness. This consciousness was One, Transcendent and

United! At each point, it was centered as the central reality of All. And I was also a part of it and it was centered in me as well!

The following, "Excerpt from a letter" that I penned was published in the Order's "in-house" journal, in the weeks that followed this dawning experience. It perhaps expresses how a young teenager processed this epiphany:

As I stepped outside into the yard at sunrise, these lines came to me, (or rather their feeling), which I tried to set down in words: The New World opened before my eyes as I felt the presence of Isis walking with me in her kingdom. As I stood and watched the solar disk rise into the domain of the morning, I felt a light dawning, rising within my heart. And my soul found rest on the trail toward the heights. And, as I stood giving a salute to the Spiritual Sun, its light covered me for the span of the whisper of a springtime breeze, caressing softly the leaves of the Kingdom. As the Sun rose into my heart, I shivered with joy. I stepped out into the dawning sun, with the light breaking through the trees and looked upon the face of Isis and saw each tiniest plant and animal, and especially the birds, as my brothers. For our Fathers are ONE! And as the mist faded away, a Voice spoke, saying, "The Light of Illumination descends not from above, but from within!"'(Adytum News Notes. Summer 1964.)

When I sensed that conscious energy linked all things and all spaces in between, I *knew* myself to be part of this Oneness. I knew, also, that this whole had a special, personal interest and caring for me. I had arrived at the answer. The answer to the question, "Where is God?"

Years later, I would be introduced to the term "Namaste." It is a Sanskrit greeting used by millions of people every day, when greeting or taking leave of each other. It translates, "The God within me, salutes the God within you!" It refers to the recognition of the indwelling Divinity seated in our heart of hearts. But, further, it is explained, that, if I am in that *One place* in me and you are in that *One place* in you, then truly, there is only One of us! We only have to seek that point within.

Where is God? Where is God not?!!

PART TWO

The Way of Initiation, General Considerations

Chapter 9
The Mystery of the Kingdom

"Seek ye first the Kingdom and all things shall be added unto you." (Matthew 6:33)

"The Kingdom of Heaven is within." (Luke 17:21)

"It is the Father's good pleasure to give you the riches of the Kingdom." (Luke 12:32)

Even a casual examination of the quotes above, taken from the Christian New Testament, reveals several important points about the mystery of the Kingdom.

First, the Kingdom is of central importance in the life of an initiate and mystic. Secondly, it is not a physical place, it is not of this world, but rather it is a state of consciousness. And finally, the Kingdom is the key to fulfillment.

There is a prayer, which came out of The Unity School of Christianity, known as The Prayer of Protection. Like the famous Breast-Plate of Saint Patrick, it is a statement of recognition of the presence of God surrounding the individual and wrapping him in the guardian power of the Divine. It ends with a truly life transforming affirmation:

"Wherever I am, God IS."

This statement is often succeeded by, "And so, all *must* be well!"

This realization of the active presence of the Indwelling Deity is one of the outcomes of the discovery of the Kingdom; also known as Illumination or Cosmic Consciousness.

Greek civilization banished the Divine to the lofty and remote environs of a Mount Olympus and this has influenced the Western World's relationship to God for over two millennia. It has divided the world into sacred and secular, heaven and earth, God and Man. The illumination experience reveals a definite knowing of the omnipresent, all-pervading influence of God. This presence unites the visible and invisible worlds.

In my meditation experience with the seventh Key of Tarot, I focused upon the term "the Receptive Intelligence." The word Qabalah can be translated as "tradition." It is derived from a Hebrew verb meaning "to receive" and therefore refers to a tradition that has been transmitted and "received" by generations of initiated teachers and students. The word "yoga" carries similar ideas. What does it mean? What is required in order that we may be receptive?

First, we must let go of our preconceptions, allowing ourselves to think, "What if?" That is, what if reality is not the way we conceive it to be? I often ask my classes, "What if there is no God? What if there is nothing after death except oblivion? Would we live our lives differently?" This examination of beliefs is helpful and, in fact, necessary to build firm foundations for life *and* for the experience of the mystical states of higher consciousness.

We must get the ego out of the way in our meditations. In the esoteric traditions, the ego is attributed to the god Mercury or Hermes, the "messenger of the gods." But, he carried another attribution also --- that of the "god of thieves." When we allow our ego to usurp the throne of the Spirit within, we have let it steal the experience of knowing that Divine Ruler. We have to "let go" of our preconceptions and become receptive to that "warrior within." We have to "let go and let God." With this surrender, the riches of the Kingdom fill us to overflowing and we know, as the song has it, "that we never walk alone."

The idea that poverty is holy, so prevalent in both the Buddhist and Catholic Orders of monks probably had its roots in a question of priorities. One who is focused upon the acquisition of material wealth and possession could, indeed, find it difficult to make spiritual attainment an important part of their life. An example of this is the story of the wealthy young man who approached Jesus and inquired what he must do to become a disciple. He was told to sell all he had and give it to the poor. It wasn't the wealth that was bad. It was a question of priorities.

On the other hand, many people will point to the saying of Paul of Tarsus that "money is the root of all evil," implying that material riches are of themselves intrinsically unspiritual. This injunction is odd, particularly since individuals or organizations that make a point of exhibiting great wealth are usually the very ones to recommend that material wealth be renounced! It has also been noted that this scripture, attributed to Paul, was perhaps intentionally mistranslated. A better translation from the Greek, would perhaps read, "Lust for money (or possessions) is the root of all evil." Lust is a compulsive, overwhelming and possessive addiction to something. A lust for anything is harmful and self-destructive. But this in no way implies that there is anything wrong with the acquisition of proper resources in order to achieve our spiritual destiny. The fruits of the Kingdom are ours. It is the "Father's good pleasure" to give them to us!

Illumination is a consciousness of abundance and prosperity.

But what of our spiritual destiny? What is the quest, the action that will enable us to claim our inheritance of the Kingdom? It is the discovery of that place within us where our soul connects with the Infinite. This "discovery of the Stone of the Wise," will not only alter our conscious viewpoint but will make the minute changes in blood chemistry and complete the subtle nerve centers so that we may transform from a "natural human" to one that is "illuminated." Remember, the treasure that we are seeking is to be found in the "jewel" within the center of our consciousness.

Chapter 10
The Three Stages

The word "initiate" means to begin. An initiation is just such a beginning; we all experience several of these. Interestingly, the month of January is named for the Roman god *Janus,* who is sometimes considered the "god of initiations." He is represented as having two faces; one looking back, reflecting upon the past, the other is gazing ahead into an uncertain future. Initiates know that to a large extent, they control their own futures by their actions and by the images that they give power to today! Our "now" is built upon the chains of causation initiated in the past and our future is directed by the decisions we make now.

In most temples of the Western Mysteries, we see representations of two pillars. These pillars symbolize the eternal "Principle of Polarity" and its manifestation as the many pairs of opposites we observe in life. One of these pairs of opposites involves time and its apparent separation into "past" and "future." In all cases, these "contraries," as the opposites are sometimes referred to, are represented in the temple or lodge room by these pieces of furniture. These are completed by an invisible third or "Middle Pillar" that represents the consciousness of the individual initiate. It is this consciousness and the lessons of its control and equilibration that is the subject of initiation.

There was a diagram in the old Golden Dawn system that was known as "The Mystical Mountain of Initiation." It depicted the mountain of attainment and the path of initiation. Up this steep and difficult path treads the candidate, through the various experiences of the grades.

Why would anyone undertake the difficult, demanding "Way of the Mysteries?" Some might suppose it is to gain power or, perhaps, intellectual fulfillment of curiosity. Others would point out, it is in the nature of a conquest of the lower nature. Still others point to those who apparently felt this call at an extremely young age and just seem to be born with this drive. But, whatever other factors or motives may be involved, there is just one reason that will safely open the Portals of the Mysteries.

Ernest (W. E.) Butler, one of the truly great teachers on this subject, points out many times that the answer is contained in the words of the promise made by a Neophyte at his initiation:

"I desire to know, that I may serve."

But what type of service and to whom is it offered? To answer these questions, we must examine more closely the Three Stages of Aspiration.

The Candidate for the Path of Initiation is set apart early on from his more materialistically oriented companions. He is, in many ways, one of the elect. The man on the street is content, most of the time, to drift along with accepted ideas put forward by the established, defining agencies of his culture. These include, but are not limited to, religious and governmental authorities, and the various scientific, academic, and economic institutions. As long as the facts of his existence do not push him out of his conventional groove or rut, he will find little incentive to question the world-view presented to him. It may never occur to him to question the reasons for suffering, war or famine, until they become personal. We are reminded of the poem which narrates how a particular individual did not protest when the Nazis came for the philosophers, teachers, Jews, Masons, trade unionists, etc. Why? Because, it was "none of his business." Then, finally, they came for him and there was no one left to protest, because he was alone!

Contrasted to this type of individual, there are, however, some who realize, as did John Donne, "And therefore never send to know for whom the bell tolls; it tolls for thee." These individuals intuitively realize they are part and parcel of humanity. What effects one – affects all. As Dion Fortune once wrote: they, "cannot accept happiness or peace for themselves while any are in grief or pain."

The Seeker

Sooner or later, this second type of person begins to seek. These "Seekers" search for the underlying meaning of existence, realizing, unconsciously, that there is a meaning, an unseen justice, and a loving purpose supporting all. They begin to look for a school or a teaching that explains and gives direction to their life. The "Ageless Wisdom" however, affirms, "if you don't find it within you shall never find it without!" With this questing, the aspirant has embarked upon the first stage of his journey, that of the "Seeker."

Impelled by forces that have their source within his soul, the Seeker sets forth, attempting to find the answer. He doesn't understand exactly what he is looking for or why it is so important. He just knows that he must find it. He will typically look at different religions and different cultures; usually quite different from those in which he was born or raised. He may become involved in what is called the naïve, lunatic, "crack-pot" fringe of occultism.

If he hasn't learned discrimination, he will likely be viewed as foolish, impractical and perhaps even mentally unstable by his stolid and orthodox friends. (I remember my older brother, asking me if I'd become a religious fanatic! I answered, "John, come on, do I <u>look</u> like a religious fanatic?")

After drifting for a period of time, be it months, years or decades, from group to group and teaching-to-teaching, he is presented with an opportunity. This opportunity is the encounter with an invitation to join his school or order, or rather, the outer vehicle for this body of teaching. The circumstances that lead him to this group may seem coincidental, but they are not. The ancient Hermeticists assure us that, "When the student is ready, the teacher will appear!" The Seeker will have been guided to this event; both by his own deep consciousness and the Great Consciousness that guards the way to the portal. I remember one individual who had been searching earnestly for several years. When moving to a new apartment, he found one item (only one) left by the prior tenants. Behind the refrigerator had fallen an introductory pamphlet of an esoteric training school – one that was just the type for which he had been searching!

The Server

We are told in the *Fama Fraternitas* that when its hero, C.R., reached the Temple in Damcar, he was received, "not as a stranger, but as one long expected." This is, in fact, not an uncommon reaction to having arrived, at last, at the right school or Order. Time and time again, I have heard a seeker describe the experience as "having come home." This is sometimes accounted for by the fact that we take initiation, life after life, in the same teaching line of the Mysteries. "Once an initiate, always an initiate!"

Having found his group, the "Seeker" becomes the "Server." And, it has been said, he will remain a Server for the rest of his life. This, indeed, is one of the tests to discern whether a candidate is ready for initiation. The Seeker who is motivated completely by what he can "get" from a teacher, teaching or organization, will move on in the endless quest for the "secret." Until the aspirant makes the determination to "give," he will never progress to the real secrets of the hidden sciences.

In the television series *Kung Fu*, I remember the hero, Kwai Chang Caine, as a young acolyte. He had just been accepted at the Shaolin Temple and was assigned to sweep the ground of the "practice yard." This is a good example of the type of service a newly accepted Server should be expected to offer in the beginning of his career in the Mysteries. "Chop wood, carry water!" as the old saying goes. The student is not qualified to offer service other than that of the routine, day-to-day, physical type. He must "earned his stripes!" He has not, at this stage, been trained for the more esoteric work. Additionally, every school or fraternity has substantial need in this area - be it time, labor or financial contributions. We must not minimize the importance of this type of service. This is one of the reasons the building-crafts, etc. are held in high honor by initiates. There is nobility in working with one's hands in service to a higher cause or purpose.

All service must be absolutely voluntary and not coerced. Initiation may not be bought. It must be earned through freely offered, dedicated service.

The hallmark of a genuine esoteric school is that this ideal of service, freely given, is evident at all levels of the organization. Each one is dedicated to serving each other, their "Higher Self," Truth and all of humanity, in whatever capacity they are qualified.

This willingness to freely give back is one of the tests of the Path. For, although each school has the right to recoup expenses for its operations, and may, therefore, set a minimum "dues," no one will ever be turned away for financial reasons. The student must therefore decide for himself what the fair value of his proper service is. It is entirely up to him. It does, however, constitute a test of his reliability, character and integrity.

The Dedicant

The third stage, encountered further along the Path and then, indeed, by only a few, concerns what is known, in the Mysteries, as the "Unreserved Dedication." The "Dedicant" is one who has decided to put the Service to the Mysteries in first place in their life. (With the exception of his duties to his family).

In order to take upon himself this dedication, the student must be willing and able, or, in the language of the Tradition, "Worthy and well qualified, duly and truly prepared."

Gareth Knight wrote, "The dedication is no thing to be lightly undertaken. It is equivalent to taking monastic vows, except that the initiate's life is lived nowadays very much in the world." (The Work of a Modern Occult Fraternity, 1962)

Chapter 11
What is Initiation?

There are two "initiations" that an aspirant will have the opportunity to receive: the Lesser and the Greater. To be complete, the Lesser must be confirmed in the physical world. The Greater initiation is always received in the spiritual realm.

The initiatory fraternities never advertise after the manner of the Madison Avenue publicity agencies. You will never find a genuine school or adept promoting themselves with full-page ads in magazines or newspapers, touting their "spiritual attainments."

In this day and age, you will find them, perhaps, with a web site, making a simple announcement of their presence, who they are and what their purpose is. This is because there is really no need for a high profile New

York agency style campaign. A Seeker who has become aware of their inner motivation for initiation sets in motion powerful currents in the inner worlds. Through the agency of subconsciousness, he will send forth a call. Like will call to like, deep will answer to deep, and the aspirant will find himself being guided to his school. Remember, "When the student is ready, the teacher will appear!" Of course, the corollary is equally true: "When the Teacher appears, the student is ready!" However, it is for a good, strong reason that it is emphasized that, "Discrimination is the first virtue of the Path." Not everyone who has unwashed feet and carries a begging bowl is sent from God.

The Teacher and the School must pass the three tests of stewardship. Have they exhibited integrity when it comes to money, power and sex? Does the school have a record of "Just men made perfect," as a result of their training or do we see a collection of skeletons falling out of their closets? Of course, the rise or fall of any school should not be judged upon the few exceptions. What must be looked for is the pattern. "By their fruits shall ye know them," is still the rule to follow.

The Lesser Initiation

When the Seeker formally unites with his school on the outer planes, he has taken the "Lesser Initiation." In the West, especially in connection with the esoteric fraternities, this normally involves ceremonial and ritual. These rituals are used to prepare the psychological, emotional and physical components of the candidate for the later experience of the Greater Initiation.

The Lesser Initiation has two basic components, a physical and a spiritual. The physical component involves the linking or entry into the group mind of the school by means of a physical ceremony. As the Catholic mass is a ceremony performed by one (the Priest) for the benefit of the many (the Congregation), the initiatory ceremony might be described as the many (the Lodge) performing a ceremony for the benefit of the one (the Candidate).

Gareth Knight, in his essay on the "Work of a Modern Occult Fraternity" (in Fortune,

1971), pointed out that during these ceremonial initiations, "…a student goes through a series of ritual dramas in which he is the main protagonist."

We should realize that these rituals do not bestow initiation. A person does not become an adept, for example, simply by going through the ceremony. Rather, the initiation ritual simply starts the process of unfoldment. As a colleague of mine once explained to me, using the analogy of photography: The spiritual forces of initiation can be likened to light. They are focused by the lens, which is the ritual, to impinge upon the prepared film of our consciousness. This produces a negative. But a photographic negative is not yet a picture until it is fully developed. It is the life experiences that we encounter with our newly sensitized consciousness that gives us an opportunity to "develop" the patterns of awakening truth that have been planted by the ceremony. The ritual merely plants the seeds, to use another analogy, in our consciousness. It is Life that is really the Initiator.

How the ritual implants these "seeds" in the subconsciousness of the candidate and how these seeds mature in his life experience will be covered in the next chapter.

"We take spiritual initiation when we become conscious of the Divine within us, and thereby contact the Divine without us." (in Fortune. *The Training and Work of an Initiate*, p.28.)

I have mentioned that currents are set in motion when the Seeker's Individuality or Higher Self begins to propel the personality, in its current incarnation, on the quest for its fraternity. This takes place in life after life. The initiate enters incarnation with a particular life lesson to accomplish. This lesson or destiny often involves the balancing of karma brought over from past lives. Sometimes, a higher initiate will enter embodiment to assist those Great Inner Adepts on the physical levels to manifest some concept or current into the race consciousness.

In the ordinary human, the entire incarnation will normally be occupied with transmuting just one major life lesson. The initiate, on the other hand, may transform or "work out" as many as four or five. Without tests, it is said, there is no triumph. Thus, an initiate can be likened to a spiritual athlete, training his chosen instrument for more proficient performance. For this reason, it sometimes seems, that the first thing to happen to the Neophyte after attaining initiation is --- he gets in trouble! This is because all of the unbalanced patterns that he has been blissfully unaware of have suddenly become energized. These patterns had been limiting his potential, causing discomfort, but were chronic rather than acute. Now they are "in his face!" He can now recognize and give attention to equilibrating them. The good news is that his positive patterns have also been energized to assist him in this work of transmutation.

For each of us, when we come into an incarnation, we spend the first part of it in recapitulation, rapidly, and in most cases recovering the lessons we have learned in our past lives with relative ease. After this, the progress becomes slower, the way rockier, as we start to break new ground.

At the point where the Individuality sends forth the soul in search of their school, we may assume the Lesser "Spiritual" Initiation has previously occurred. External aid will be made available to the earnest student when he requires it. The story of the young Paul Foster Case furnishes us with a good example of this phenomenon.

Case had been clairaudient from an early age, receiving the guidance of an "inner teacher" in his studies of Tarot and Qabalah. We are told that he was walking down a street in downtown Chicago. Paul would be performing in a concert and was now wrestling with his options for a career.

On his way to this performance, he was approached by a complete stranger who called him by name and revealed to him many facts about his life that were impossible for him to know! The stranger introduced himself as Dr. Fludd and explained to Paul's satisfaction that he too was a student of the same mysterious inner teacher that instructed Paul. Dr. Fludd told Paul that he had been sent to meet him and to give him an important message. The essence of the message was that Paul was now at a very important crossroads in his life. He could choose to pursue a career as a professional musician and he would achieve a degree of success that would provide a comfortable standard of living. He would accumulate more than the average share of this world's goods. Or, on the other hand, he could dedicate his life to transmitting the Ageless Wisdom of the Tarot and Qabalah in a new manner, suitable for twentieth century humanity. If he chose this second option, he would accomplish a great good, helping many seekers. He would achieve little fame in his lifetime. He was also assured that although he would accumulate little in worldly renown or goods, in the end, he would not starve to death!

Those who would obtain the experience of the Lesser Initiation, the finding of the "right" school and entering into the service of the "Hierarchy of Light," often ask how to proceed. I would answer, never underestimate the power of a clear, emotionally charged aspiration. Send your call into the Inner and it shall be answered. Remember, any clear mental image, repeatedly held and focused with desire will manifest itself as an actual condition or event.

Chapter 12
The Greater Initiation

In the last chapter, we discussed the two aspects of the Lesser Initiation. Achieving this experience, one can consider themselves an initiate. Some confusion occurs, now and then, by the different uses of this term. Let us be clear in our definitions.

Dion Fortune defines an initiate as "one in whom the Higher Self, the Individuality, has coalesced with the personality and actually entered into incarnation in the physical body." *(Training and Work of an Initiate, p.34)* Cyril Scott, writing under the pen name of "A Pupil" in his *The Initiate* trilogy, refers to his hero Justin Morgan Haig, in much the same way.

However, in the school in which I was trained, and in the sense used in this book, an initiate is one who has achieved the Greater

Initiation. And the term I use to identify such an individual is, instead, an "adept."

Paul Case once defined an adept as "one who has achieved *conscious immortality*. This experience is marked by the state known as "illumination," awakening, or "Cosmic Consciousness." It is the result of minute adjustments of the blood chemistry and metabolism which brings these functions to a much greater degree of efficiency. These changes are achieved by spiritual, alchemical techniques, initiated by the individual's conscious use of imagery. As an outcome of these practices, certain organs that are normally found in natural humans, but in rudimentary form, are evolved and completed. Nerve currents are activated causing an increased functioning of the seven alchemical metals, known as "chakras" in the East. As a result, the fusing of the Melatonin or "brain-sand" found in the pineal body forms a citrine colored, cubical crystal. This is the organ of spiritual vision. It is referred to, symbolically, in the Bible and in Masonic literature as the completion of the Sanctum Sanctorum or "Holy of Holies" of King Solomon's Temple.

This crystal, which is also referred to in Alchemical literature as the "Philosopher's Stone," allows the brain to interrupt and mediate high-tension currents of the astral/etheric planes. These currents would destroy the vehicles of individuals who have not achieved this transformation. This condition opens the personality consciousness to a complete and continual recognition of the level of consciousness functioning at the level of the Individuality or Higher Self. Thus, one who has realized this awakening may say, with Jesus, "My Father and I are One!" And he may say this as a statement of verified fact.

In the Qabalah, this state is referenced by the Hebrew word for stone, nba or ABN (ehben). When analyzed, this term is a symbolic combination of two Hebrew words, "Ab" (AB) – father, and, "ben" (BN) – son.

Ab + Ben = Abben or Ehben

This Greater Initiation is the goal of the Great Work. It is sometimes asked if we can achieve this awakening, this initiation, on the Inner Planes of consciousness, say, during sleep, without having realized it in waking consciousness. The answer is obviously "NO!" The result of this experience is illumination. If we are unaware of this awakened state of consciousness, on all levels, then we have not experienced it!

While, as Dion Fortune points out, "This Great Initiation is invariably gone through out of body," *(Training and work of an Initiate, p.34.)* it is an experience that intimately involves the body. By it, an aspirant is transformed from "Homo Naturalis" into "Homo Adeptus."

This initiation, as I have pointed out, is not conveyed by a ritual or ceremony. The ceremonial process of the Lesser Mysteries does, however, prepare the vehicles of consciousness to receive this experience.

Chapter 13
The Lesser Mysteries

The system used by the initiatory fraternities of the West is generally divided into two broad, functional classifications (There is a third, but it is the province of the Supreme Mysteries of the Masters, which is, for the most part, beyond the scope of this book).

These two classifications are generally referred to as The Lesser and The Greater Mysteries. The Lesser, which is also known as "the Mysteries of the Microcosm" or "the Mysteries of Isis," comprise the work of the "First Order" of the Fraternity of the Hidden Light.

This stage begins the preparatory work that must precede the descent of the Higher Self into normal waking consciousness. The normal personality/physical body complex of the average individual is similar to a house that has been built up over the years, in reaction to the requirements of a growing family. It really has no overall set of architectural plans, and no idea what it would look like when completed. When the Aspirant begins the disciplines and practices of initiated work, he gradually replaces, re-balances, and rebuilds the house of his personality. This is done so that, one day, it may become a fit temple for the manifestation of the Higher Self, and the Spirit he really is.

The initiate has several advantages in this "renovation" process. First, he is proactive rather than reactive. He does not let the events, challenges or circumstances of his day-to-day existence dictate his action. He has realized, at least intellectually, the nature of the law of causation and utilizes it in ever-greater degree to aid in the process of regeneration. Secondly, he has a "blue-print," an "architectural plan." This Master Pattern may also be considered to be road map of the Kingdom of which he is preparing to become the conscious ruler.

Following this plan he may avoid the distortions and imbalances that plague his uninitiated brethren. How often have I heard sincere spiritual seekers mistakenly affirm that they have no need for a group or school or a system. They declare that their "inner guides" will tell them what to do. They will follow the methods or techniques that feel right for them. In the very great majority of these cases, the individual has not developed the inner discrimination to distinguish between true guidance and the lower astral nature masquerading as such.

It is an accepted fact that our mind will tend to repeat actions and patterns that have proven to be successful in the past. This is usually called the "learning effect." However, as the individual matures, unless he possesses remarkable insight, he will tend more and more to limit his options and opportunities. He will refrain from taking new, original or creative initiatives. (The so-called, "You can't teach an old dog new tricks!") It is suggested that this is one reason we learn so much faster and more easily in earlier life than later. We have cut a groove, very deep, into our consciousness by repeating responses of thinking and action, until it becomes a habitual rut. This results in an increasing imbalance in our natures that inhibits our ability to adapt, change and learn. This must be consciously changed in order for the personality to become the vehicle for higher realizations. The higher, mystical mentation of the illuminated consciousness, together with the more powerful astral currents that accompany it, cannot be supported by the personality/body that is evolved through this "profane" life experience. Thus, Jesus tells us that we must, "…become as a little child…" before we can enter the Kingdom of Heaven.

The individual who, relying on his personal preferences, and doing "what feels right," will naturally gravitate toward his strengths. If he has a good intellect, he will tend to pursue those disciplines and methods that are designed to develop the intellect, while neglecting the emotional or artistic nature resulting in an even greater imbalance. This will result in the dry-as-dust theoretician who can tell you how many angels, indeed, would fit on the head of a pin, but cannot make use of any of this information for self-perfection.

On the other hand, we find those folks who believe that the only way to God is the "Way of the Heart." Now Love *is* the most powerful force in the universe, but this great power tends to be reduced to a pastel sentimentality by one so imbalanced. In order for the true power of unconditional love to manifest, the personality must become the balanced vehicle for the higher consciousness. If the expression of love is conditional; that is, if there are "strings attached", then it is not given freely and this is a sign of an unbalanced "delivery system."

Artistic individuals will tend to pursue the path in this direction and, unless they are careful, will tend to neglect the intellectual disciplines that will give lasting value to their expression. Instead of becoming vehicles for the "True, the Good, and the Beautiful," they will manifest the "politically correct, the nice and the pretty!"

For these reasons, the genuine esoteric fraternities ask all aspirants, no matter what their prior accomplishments, to begin as a humble Neophyte and to proceed, grade by grade, through the balancing and building processes of the Lesser Mysteries. The truly advanced, "Old Soul," will, without exception, be willing to sacrifice any psychic attainments or worldly renown they may have achieved, in one or another areas, and to begin again. In this way, they temporarily set aside their "gifts" and status while they "build the Temple, not made with hands." They know that when the adytum is completed, they will be rightly entitled to the "the Master's Word" and their spiritual gifts, enhanced by the process of equilibration, will be available to be placed in use upon the altar of the Higher Life.

The method of this balancing is to build upon the natural strengths of the aspirant rather than repressing those areas where they possess gifts and talents. Therefore, the artist is not directed to repress their skills in manifesting imagery, but instead, is led to develop the skills and techniques of the intellect that results in an enhanced expression through discipline. Psychics, who typically find their skills submerged into abeyance during this process, eventually discover that these abilities have returned with greater vividness, power and depth, but now they have greater control of their use than they had ever dreamt of possessing.

The purpose of this process is to perfect the qualities of consciousness through which the Higher Self may manifest. These "qualities" may be categorized as the physical and or etheric, deep consciousness, intellectual, and emotional natures. During the Candidate's journey through the First Order, each of these components of the personality is selectively stimulated and equilibrated. This is accomplished by a balanced application of three methods: ritual, meditation, and study.

Each stage is initiated by the experience of an "Attunement." This is a carefully constructed ritual through which the keynote of a particular stage is invoked. The resulting force is concentrated in the aura of the candidate through the principle of resonance. This is equivalent to the well-known phenomenon whereby a tuning fork is struck and causes the corresponding note on a piano to vibrate. However, this is just one level of the effect the ritual has upon the aspirant.

The effect of the various symbolic stimuli upon a prepared consciousness must also be considered. During these ceremonies, all of the sensory input is calculated to produce a potent suggestion in the subconscious of the candidate. This suggestion targets and stimulates the relevant area of consciousness.

We must remember, however, that the attuning of the consciousness doesn't end with the effects of the ceremony. Daily meditational exercises are undertaken that produce a deepening and stabilization of the realizations connected with this awakening.

Meditation, in this tradition, is different from the "Zazen" of the Zen school. It is also not the mere relaxation techniques that became popular in the West during the last quarter of the twentieth century. It is the active pursuit of a chain of ideas, focused around a central subject or concept. This process has been compared to fishing. (This is appropriate, since the Hebrew letter "tzaddi", which means "fishhook" is associated with the activity of meditation in the Qabalah.) The hook is baited with an initial subject to be focused upon, usually in the form of a question. It is cast into the water of the deep consciousness. Fish after fish is pulled up, each forming a link in the symbolic chain of realization. After a "successful" meditation, the meditator finds himself to be the recipient of a new concept or understanding that was not present before he initiated the process!

Meditation must be the foundation of any system of spiritual awakening, for by it we form the symbolic bridge that allows the power and revelation to flow from the wellspring of inner consciousness. It is said that as a result of this process, we arrive at the certain realization that, instead of doing the meditating, we find it is we who have been meditated. We become part of the universal, cosmic process!

Paul Case once wrote that, "Of all the techniques available to man for spiritual development, the most powerful is ritual." Rituals are used in group settings in the Mysteries. The aspirant is also given individual ritualistic practices that serve to awaken particular capabilities. Rituals, in these forms, are a key part of the methodology associated with the Way of Return, which may be described as an extremely powerful discipline associated with "practical psychology."

Study allows the candidate to form an intellectual framework and to develop understanding and to effectively communicate those realizations revealed during meditation and in moments of inspiration.

The road map or "Master Pattern" upon which the Initiatory Path of the Western Mysteries is generally based is the Qabalistic Tree of Life. In the next chapter, we will discuss the major components of this great symbol as it applies to the initiatory process.

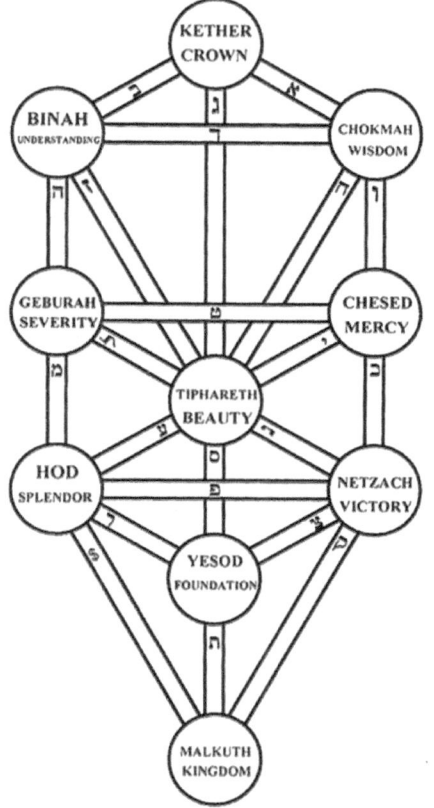

The Qabalistic Tree of Life

Figure One

Chapter 14
The Yoga of the West

Dion Fortune in her classic work on the Tree of Life, *The Mystical Qabalah*, coined a term for the secret wisdom of the Western Tradition. She called it "The Yoga of the West." Yoga means "yoking" and is taken to mean that collection of doctrines, techniques and disciplines that lead to enlightenment. As such the term defines practical mysticism. Qabalah and yoga do have many similarities. The differences are primarily due to the application of techniques that have been adapted to cultural factors. The Eastern disciplines were developed in societies that allowed its mystical practitioners to withdraw into communities or ashrams. There, uninterrupted regimens might be followed non-stop in the quest for spiritual awakening.

In the West, with its emphasis on "being in the world," if not of it, a different approach had to be developed. A system evolved that afforded its devotees the opportunity to walk between the worlds. Thus, in the Qabalah it is said that although one may go to the mountaintop to receive mystical truth, it is not really obtained until it can be proven in the marketplace!

In the Hermetic Qabalah, we find an assortment of techniques developed over two millennia that have been used by initiates to develop their control of consciousness, to modify their physical vehicles, to understand the cosmos and to enhance their awareness of the Divine both within and without. This clear perception of the nature of reality is what we have referred to as Greater Initiation.

In the legends found in the classical works of the Qabalah, we learn that it was originally taught to an infant humanity by the angels. Before we dismiss this story entirely or conjure images of winged emissaries from heaven, whispering in the ears of the holy scribes, let us consider a few points.

The word "angel" literally means, "messenger of God." It is used in the *Book of Revelation*, for example to refer to the leaders or ministers of the "Seven Churches that are in Asia."

In the esoteric tradition we are told of the "Elder Brethren," who were from an earlier life-wave, assisting ancient humanity. This seems to be supported by archeological evidence that suggests that emissaries from earlier, but comparatively advanced civilizations that were destroyed by flood were perhaps those that taught our ancestors.

And then there is a story in the Qabalistic writings of the *Zohar* that could be interpreted to suggest extra-terrestrial influence!

Take your pick. The point is that for most legends of this type, there usually is some basis in fact. The foundational concept is this: the Qabalah and the initiatory system of the West were received. It was not "home grown." It is relevant that the word "Qabalah" which means "tradition" comes from the Hebrew verb

"Qebel" which translates "to receive." One of the names for this body of knowledge is, in fact, "the received tradition."

Historically, it became known by these terms about the seventh century of the Common Era. However, it is known to have existed both in oral and written form much earlier. At one time it was called "Merkabah," which means "of the Chariot." This referred to the mystical vehicle, the "Chariot of God" mentioned in the Book of Ezekiel. Much of this literature concerns the altering or elevating of the consciousness of the practitioner to mystical states of perception. This process accessed the visionary road of the chariot of consciousness, through the seven heavens, to the Throne of God. This, of course, was based upon earlier Chaldee initiatory practices involving the famous stepped pyramids known as ziggurats. Each level corresponded to a different planet, god or goddess and level of consciousness. The order of these attributions and the colors assigned along with them have come down to us as the traditional order of the sephiroth on the Qabalistic Tree of Life.

This connection is even more obvious when we examine a diagram of the Tree presented as concentric circles, (see Figure Two). This version is traditionally considered to be much older than the more familiar "three pillar" arrangement.

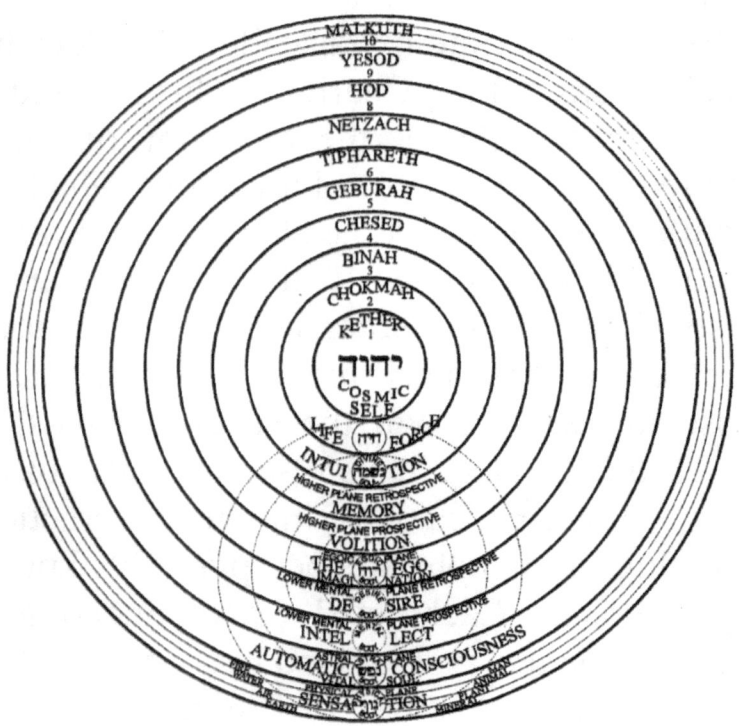

Qabalist Diagram of Concentric Circles

Figure Two

What we're looking at may be interpreted as a "bird's eye view" of the ziggurat from above! Among the ancient Chaldee, the candidate would be ceremonially initiated at each level, progressing up the symbolic "mountain of initiation" until he communed with the highest level.

This physical/psychic ceremonial system evolved into a meditative, astral skrying system in the days of Merkabah mysticism. (As an aside, there was a group in the early 1970's in Los Angeles that attempted to revive this system. They went by the name," The Work of the Chariot.")

According to the late Aryeh Kaplan, we may also find roots of the Qabalah in the "School of the Prophets" founded by Samuel on Mount Carmel as mentioned in the Old Testament. Later Plotinus, and other Neo-Platonists influenced the roots of the Qabalah.

The 13th century is considered to be the "Golden Age" of Qabalah. In areas such as Safed in Galilee, whole communities were given over to the study of Qabalah. Tales are told of young Jewish mystics dancing in processions through the streets. There were all night meetings held in cemeteries where the aspirant would meditate while either sitting or lying upon the graves of famous Qabalistic sages. It was thought that they could more easily attune themselves with the vibrations of these great teachers under these conditions.

The synagogues of these groups, some of which may still be seen today, were distinctive. Often they were painted a light blue and were round in shape. Many times they would have protective verses, invocations and talismans, etc. from the *Sepher Ratziel* and other books of Qabalistic magic written on the walls. Frequently, these verses were written in one of the "mystical alphabets" that may be found, for example, in *The Greater Key of Solomon*.

In 1492 – Columbus sailed the ocean blue

The year 1492 A.D. holds much historical significance in European history. Most school children will quickly remind you that it was in this year that Isabella and Ferdinand of Spain granted Christopher Columbus' petition to outfit three small ships, the Nina, the Pina and the Santa Maria and sail across the Atlantic in search of a trade route to India.

For the purposes of our study, another proclamation made by "their most Catholic Majesties of Spain" that same year was more important. This was the decision to expel the Jews from their kingdom.

During the fifteenth century, there arose in Spain, notably in the cities of Toledo and Seville, great universities. These were centers of learning for all the arts and sciences, especially philosophy and mysticism. Here the great mystics of Christendom met the Sufis of Islam and the Qabalists of Judaism. A remarkable cross-fertilization took place with noteworthy advances in the arts and sciences.

The ruling political powers drove the Moors back across Gibraltar as dramatized in the novel "El Cid." And in 1492, the Jews were expelled from Spain and the Inquisition suppressed mystics and other progressive thinkers.

But Spain's great loss was a great gain for the rest of Europe, especially Florence where Jewish mystics were eagerly solicited and accepted. For the most part, they were highly educated, skilled and gifted. Many historians, Frances Yates among them, postulate that this was a major factor in the spread of the Renaissance across Europe. One of the rulers who was instrumental in the acceptance of these Jewish immigrants, was Cosmo de Medici of Florence. He actively recruited these philosophers to help in the establishment of his Platonic Academy. He also collected a vast number of ancient manuscripts for his library. It was in Florence that the works of Aristotle and Hermes Trismegistus were first translated into Latin. It was here also that the Christian and Hermetic Qabalah were born.

Chapter 15
The Master Pattern

Any study of initiation in the Western Tradition must include a discussion of the symbol known as The Tree of Life. Indeed, this diagram from the Qabalah is central to the subject. It shows relationships existing between two aspects of the universal creative process, the Macrocosm, and its correspondences in the consciousness of the individual, the Microcosm. The Tree also functions as a roadmap for the Paths of Initiation.

The Tree is composed of ten aspects or expression known as the sephiroth (singular – sephirah). This Hebrew word is usually translated as "emanations." Twenty-two lines, known as paths connect these sephiroth and chart their relationships. Taken together the sephiroth and the paths comprise what is known as "The 32 Paths of Wisdom."

Most importantly for our present study, is the fact that many of the major initiatory orders of the West organize their grades of awakening or degrees around this diagram. This is particularly true of the great inner plane order for which the Fraternity of the Hidden Light is an outer vehicle. This order is known as the "True and Invisible Order."

These grades or levels of attunement proceed from the manifested plane of existence, the one we experience with our everyday consciousnesses, stage-by-stage, to ever more subtle levels, progressing toward the essential reality of the All. The final goal of initiation and enlightenment is often stated as "Union with God." Seers have consistently observed that Deity and humanity are essentially the same. Similarly, esoteric tradition proclaims the essential royalty of the common man. As initiates, we strive to become conscious participants in the Kingdom of the manifest, to become citizens, rather than subjects, to enter into the joy of our divine heritage, here and now.

This world of form that we see about us appears to be full of darkness, opacity and opposition. But when we learn to penetrate beneath surface appearances and learn to see into it, we find that it is a harmonious flow of light and luminescence, an ineffable manifestation that is identical to the Aur of the Jews or the L.V.X. of the Rosicrucians.

In the Bible, we read, "If our eye be single, our body will be full of light." This is the eye of the illuminated mind that sees the Unity of the All and recognizes that the reality composing the material universe is that of the Divine Spirit.

It is from this experience of the transcendence of the everyday manifested universe that the Path of Initiation differs from many of the orthodox religions. They, to a greater or lesser degree, conceive of the world of matter as opposed to the spiritual, as evil and as a condition from which they seek to escape.

The Tree of Life is, in fact, a symbol of our total selfhood and real identity! The initiatory experiences that result in union with the

Individuality which characterizes the Greater Initiation comes through an awakened intuitive nature. It is through this level only that the personality may grasp the inner truth behind the outer words, phrases and images that are used to train the consciousness for this experience.

The graded practices undertaken by an initiate are designed to gradually increase the personality's ability to handle the higher vibratory rates of consciousness. This is accomplished by developing the capacity of the inner centers to transform these energies. During this process, the initiate must be attentive in recognizing any residual negative patterns, related to those areas that are being awakened, that will obstruct the complete realization of the expression of the higher nature.

Using the "doctrine of correspondences" the aspirant attunes his consciousness on the lower levels, which, in turn, balances and awakens corresponding higher octaves. Attunement with one level will reveal correspondences of the same frequency at a higher octave on the "cosmic keyboard." The initiate forms links of realization that can facilitate conscious identification with areas that transcend his normal day-to-day perceptions.

So, let us briefly examine the components of the "Master Pattern" that will guide the aspirant through this process of initiation. There are ten major aspects diagramed on the Tree of Life. These are referred to as the sephiroth. These mark stages of expression in the creative process as the Life Energy proceeds from origin to manifestation. If these stages are followed in reverse, back to the Source, we have a map of the process of initiation. But, above all, remember the Tree represents the initiate, both in his realized and latent states of beingness.

The Veils of the Absolute

The Qabalah states that there are three "Veils of Negative Existence" that form a backdrop to the creative process. Since the Absolute is infinite, we cannot comprehend it with the finite, reasoning mind. Adepts and higher mystics may "apprehend" (that is, touch the essence) in the most exalted of mystical revelations. For the rest of us, we can make use of symbols in much the same way as a mathematician does in an algebraic equation to learn something of these most abstract levels, these levels before the beginning.

Ain

Paul Case tells us that the Hebrew word "Ain," is commonly used as an adverb of interrogation, "where?" He further suggests that it asks the question, "Where did the Universe come from?" and, "...where is it going to?"

As a noun, it means "nothing" or "no-thing." The first thing that we can infer about the Source of everything is that it cannot be defined as anything. It is not finite. From our point of view it is conditionally and continually No-Thing.

Qabalists point out that the initial letter of Ain is the first letter of the Hebrew alphabet, "Aleph." In connection with the first veil of the Absolute, it is the so-called "Dark Aleph." The "Bright Aleph" being attributed to the path connecting the first two Sephiroth. Concerning this Dark Aleph, the French adept, Eliphas Levi wrote:

Unity may be conceived as universal, producing and embracing all numbers, having therefore no duality, a unity without numbers, absolutely necessary and incomprehensible.

Thus, the Ain stands for pure spiritual potential.

Ain Suph

The second veil of the Absolute is designated as the "Ain Suph," or the "Limitless." Note that the first word of the Ain Suph is identical with the name of the veil preceding it and carries the same meaning of "absolute potential" in the name of the second veil.

Paul Case points out in his writings, that Ain Suph may be translated as "not perishable" or "never ending." Thus, we may infer that it carries the meaning of "eternal" and "everlasting."

The second veil is associated with all the ideas of "no-limits." Obviously, any definition that places a limitation on the "All" is necessarily inaccurate. We cannot limit the infinite!

Ain Suph Aur

The third veil adds the concept of "Aur," which is Hebrew for "Light." Thus, Ain Suph Aur may be translated as "The Limitless Light." Modern physics confirms what the Ageless Wisdom has taught for centuries, namely, that all manifestation is based upon electro-magnetic activity. Light is infinite in its manifestation. It cannot be limited to the narrow wavelength band to that humans are able to perceive. Everything we see, touch, or sense is truly composed of light. In addition, those wavelengths that we have not, as yet, developed instruments to perceive are also composed of light.

We may image this veil as being made of innumerable points of light, a "Great Sea of Living Light." Each point is omnipotent, omniscient, omnipresent and omni-benevolent!

It is this Limitless Light that swirls and concentrates itself into the *Primal Point* which gives rise to the first sephirah called Kether, "The Crown."

Chapter 16
The Ladder of Lights

The physical manifestations of our daily lives are determined by the images that are held in the inner planes of consciousness. To change our lives, we must first change the patterns on which they are based. The more perfectly these inner patterns mirror Universal Truth, the more aligned we will become with the forces of the Cosmos, resulting in lives filled with joy, peace and true success. Most people have no overall plan, or at best, only a fragmentary one, so that almost any organized system would be an improvement. There are many groups, many systems that offer guidelines for living. Initiates have the advantage of having the opportunity to adopt the pattern used by adepts to perfect their own vehicles.

Most of humanity is traveling along the path to self-realization using the slow and painful method of trial and error. Initiates must also travel this same path, but they are made aware that a few advanced souls have already made this journey and, through compassion, have returned to give us a road map. The aspirant must still make the journey himself, he will acquire muscles (and blisters) along the way, but using this map will give him a great advantage over those who refuse to believe that such a map exists. He knows where he is going and by studying the map he discovers how to get there. This map is the Tree of Life.

This "Master Pattern" also functions like a circuit diagram, showing the flow of forces from inner, spiritual, and causative levels to outer, personal, and physical levels. It shows the aspirant relationships between aspects of his own consciousness and those described in all other major esoteric symbol systems. Like a Rosetta Stone of consciousness, it helps to decode the truth behind many systems of esoteric teachings. No wise man claims to know "all about the Tree." No one can. For the initiate who chooses to follow this path, the

Tree of Life will become a meditational mandala, blueprint, and source of study in myriad forms for years to come.

The vast complexity of the Tree comes from its ability to correlate with so many different systems (astrological, alchemical, or those of Egyptian, Celtic, and Christian systems as well, among others) and to show what lessons each teaches about the place of humanity in the Universal Order. At the same time, it has a beautiful simplicity that lies in its ability to organize volumes of seemingly unrelated facts into one usefully coordinated system, giving us a method whereby man may regain his Divine birthright.

As we explore the main components of the sephiroth we will try to build a framework for our studies. Thus, we will limit this discussion to a brief introduction. The goal of our study is not the empty mental exercise of trying to compile the longest list of attributions; the goal is to become the Tree.

The Sephiroth

1. *KETHER:* (Keth' r) – "The Crown"

The first outpouring of the Limitless Light, the Primal Will, the Ancient of Days, the Cosmic Unity. In the Macrocosm it is the Godhead, Source of all existence. In the Microcosm it symbolizes the Divine spark that unites us with the Ultimate Deity, that Great Unmanifest which can neither be named nor defined. It is also called "the Beginning of the Whirlings." Kether is the root of the Tree of Life.

2. *CHOKMAH:* (Hok' mah) – "Wisdom"

The Supernal Father, the Seed. While Kether is considered the first aspect of positive existence and is symbolized by a point, the simplest geometrical concept, Chokmah shows the next stage – direction. Direction indicates movement with purpose. Its symbol is the line. It represents absolute potential, energy not yet restricted by form: explosive, all-powerful, unbridled expansion. Chokmah is head of the

Masculine Pillar of Force. Astrologically it corresponds to the Zodiac.

3. ***BINAH:*** (Bee' nah) – "Understanding"

The Divine Mother, the Cosmic Womb, the Great Sea. The third sephirah heads the Feminine and Form side of the Tree. As the projective power of the line of Chokmah starts to move, the magnetic Love of Binah attracts and shapes this projection into a curve, creating the structure of space. The limiting aspect of Binah is seen again in its correspondence with Saturn and time (Chronos). In the Microcosm, Binah is the seat of the *Neshamah,* or Divine Soul, the Holy Spirit of Christian symbolism. She is the source of intuition. She confines, directs and concentrates the force of Chokmah, and thereby is the Mother of all creation.

4. ***CHESED:*** (Hes'ed) – "Mercy"

Compassion, anabolism, the force that builds, memory. This sephirah is the highest of the Triangle of Individuality. To it is attributed the planet Jupiter. Jupiter/Zeus was the king of the Greek Olympian pantheon and Chesed has the image of the "just King," the beneficent and wise ruler, administrating the Kingdom according to the laws of the Cosmos. It is also the level assigned to the Chasidim, the Lords of Compassion. Microcosmically, Chesed is attributed to memory, not the personal memory, but the Memory of the Cosmos. At the level of Return symbolized by Chesed, Man "remembers" who God is and the nature of the Universe. He knows why he was created and understands the purpose of his life. True compassion is always in balance with a firm Justice that is represented by the next sephirah, Geburah.

5. ***GEBURAH:*** (Gee bur' ah) – "Severity," and also ***Pachad*** – "Fear" and ***Din*** – "Justice"

These titles describe the three ways that man usually reacts to God's power. Early man viewed God with awe or fear. He attempted to propitiate the forces he feared in the hope that they would favor him. The more "advanced" man views the universe as a huge and severe mechanism that is governed by cold unresponsive forces that smash the person unlucky enough to run afoul of their inexorable rule. This, sadly, is the viewpoint that is prevalent today. It is called Materialism, a belief which leads to placing all of one's efforts into acquiring possessions. The assumption is that the physical world is all that there is. It views the outer world of effects as the sum total of reality and remains in ignorance of the inner world of cause. In reality, contrary to Materialism's goals, the person who has the most toys is not necessarily the winner. To a few in every generation, there comes a vision of the Higher. To those, the manifested universe is the luminous image of its Creator and they see that all laws are manifestation of the principles of Cosmic Justice and Love.

Geburah corresponds to Mars, action, law and to catabolism, the breaking down of the old so that the new may be built. In man, the Geburah aspect manifests as the power of volition, purpose or will. We have no need to develop will power. True Will is a cosmic power, not a personal characteristic and is exhaustlessly available to us. In early (and intermediate) stages of our training, it does appear that the discipline required is a function of our own will power. However, when we accept the reality that our will is an aspect of the Universal, that we have no will "save to do the Will of Him who sent me," the power of the universe shall flow through us. Adepts all report that once we reach the stage where we can truly see, we will know that no matter how it appeared at the time, our progress on the Path has not been a result of our personal pushing from below, but is caused by the gentle pull of a benevolent hand from above.

6. *TIPHARETH:* (Tif'er eth) – "Beauty"

The Ego, I, Christ Consciousness, the Messiah, the Sacrificed God, the True King. Macrocosmically, Tiphareth corresponds to the Sun, the center of consciousness that makes all life in our Solar System possible. Microcosmically, it refers to the Individuality, the real Self that is an extension of the Solar Logos, the Self that reincarnates again and again until the Destiny of Perfection is achieved and identity with the Logoidal consciousness is complete. It is important that we make it clear that this goal is not equivalent to a loss of identity (as some mistakenly interpret the Eastern teaching of Nirvana). The

Path of Initiation is not for those who seek "divine oblivion." On the contrary, we are told by those who have gone before us that the only loss is that the false self (ego, vanity), now realized for what it is – a very small part of the whole. With this realization comes direct knowledge and awareness of the very uniqueness and scope of the True SELF.

7. *NETZACH:* (Net' zok) – "Victory"

Corresponding to the Green Ray, to Venus and the ancient element of Fire, Netzach is the seat of the emotions and the desire force – which according to the alchemists must be purified and turned white. There is a mistaken idea among some spiritual aspirants that they must achieve a state of "desirelessness." What must be killed out, in reality, are the misinterpretations of desire. No desire originates at the level of personality. All desires – we repeat – ALL DESIRES – are Divine in origin! No matter how distorted, how selfish, how base, they seem to us, they are all rooted in the One Self's desire for unity with Its creation. The desire is pure. Our methods of fulfilling the desire, however, often need to be re-examined and restructured, and our selfish interpretations may have to be sacrificed until the true holiness of desire is realized.

Without Desire we would have no motivation and would become "aspirationally dead." We would become like a boat in the ocean without oars or sail or motor. With no means of propulsion, we would simply drift with the currents. Remember the sages tell us "Inflame yourself with prayer!" A fiery emotion is a prerequisite for spiritual advancement.

8. *HOD:* (Hode) – "Splendor"

Hod corresponds to Mercury and the Orange Ray. The eighth sephirah is the complement of the seventh. While Netzach concerns the emotions of our conscious mind, Hod is the sphere of thoughts or the intellect. It is also attributed to the ancient element of Water. Let us examine this Water and its properties. Physical water can be solid, as ice. It can be a gas when agitated by heat, as steam. As a liquid, water has no form of its own but will assume the form of any mold into which it is poured. Just so with thoughts; they will take the form of images that are supplied by the consciousness of Man. These "forms" have a greater or lesser permanency depending on their relation to archetypal images, and the duration of the period that these images are held. If an image is reinforced by ritual and performed with knowledge, it can be remarkably persistent.

Another important analogy is revealed by the qualities of reflection. Water, when disturbed, distorts an image. The mind of Man, when agitated or disturbed, cannot truly reflect inner reality. Only when the pool of consciousness is stilled can the true reflection of the One Self be perceived. One of the purposes of meditation is to "still the pool."

9. **YESOD:** (Yeh – sed) – "Foundation"

Seat of the Vital Soul, Yesod corresponds to the Moon, and along with Tiphareth, to the Purple Ray. Macrocosmically, this sephirah refers to the Astral Plane, that state or vibration that is contiguous to the physical plane. The Astral Plane holds the molds or matrixes of the physical. Most of our imagery never, fortunately, comes to fruition in physical manifestation. That is why one of the titles of the physical world is "Cholem Yesodoth" or "Breaker of the Foundations." Microcosmically, Yesod is assigned to the subconsciousness.

10. **MALKUTH:** (moll – kooth) – "Kingdom," also called "the Bride."

Macrocosmically, this is the manifested universe, the Garden of Eden, the Fruit of the Tree. Microcosmically, it is the physical body, the Temple, the "Harp of Ten Thousand Strings." The concepts of the kingdom restored to the True King (Tiphareth), and the Bridegroom (also Tiphareth) rescuing his Bride, are metaphors that allude to the union of the personality with the Higher Self. Without this union, man identifies only with his mortal, transitory shell. The Hebrew word for the physical body is "Guph." From it we get the term "goofy" for one who is only a body, a dull clod.

Malkuth is normally subdivided into four quadrants (see diagram), each bearing the symbol of one of the four elements of the Ancients. These "elements" refer to components or states of matter rather than the classification of types of substances according to their atomic number.

Malkuth

Thus, in physical terms, Earth ($\triangledown$) refers to solids, Water ($\triangledown$) to liquids, Air ($\triangle$) to gases, and Fire ($\triangle$) to radiant energy. Those same qualities are seen in people who are as stable as Earth, as flexible as Water, as active as Air, as strong as Fire.

The redemption of Malkuth, both microcosmically and macrocosmically, is one of the primary goals of the Great Work.

This is the merest introduction to the Tree of Life. Although the following chapter will provide additional material, the student who is earnest in his desire to learn more is encouraged to refer to the contact information at the end of this book and enroll in "The Threshold" and "The Path of Return," courses for a more in-depth examination.

In the next chapter, we will look at some of the patterns and relationships on the Tree of Life.

Chapter 17
Patterns on the Tree

To understand the Tree of Life and how it is intimately related to the process of initiation, the sephiroth must be considered in relation to each other. These "patterns" on the Tree help us penetrate more deeply into the mysteries of the initiatic path.

The Tree of Life can be considered in terms of configurations referred to as pillars and triangles.

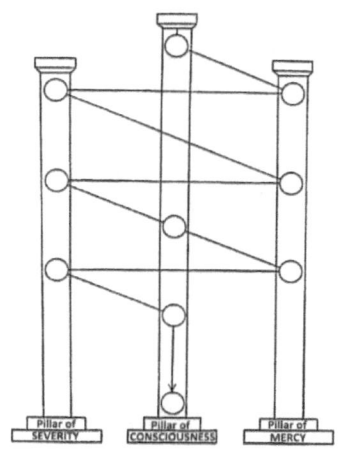

Figure Three

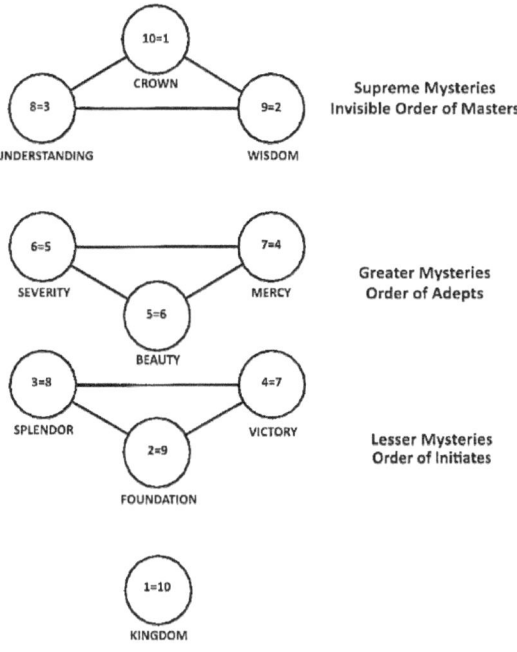

Figure Four

Referencing Figure Three, we see how it is organized into three pillars. As we have pointed out previously, these pillars structure or divide the sephiroth on the Tree into two opposite columns, mediated by a third one down the center called the "Middle Pillar." The two outer pillars can be said to represent male and female, father and mother, force and form, past and future, etc. The middle pillar of Consciousness can then be said to represent, respectively, the Androgyne, the Child, Mind, and the Present.

Another approach to examining the Tree is via the relationships created by the triangular configurations, (Figure Four). When the Ain Suph Aur centers itself in the "beginning of the whirlings," this concentration produces the "Primal Point" of Kether. It is "the circle whose center is everywhere and circumference is nowhere." This is the Crown. It is said that the entire Tree, as an archetype, is instantly established at this point and is symbolized by a "lightning flash." This is the archetypal or "Tree in Germ," and gives rise to the saying, "Malkuth is in Kether and Kether is in Malkuth, but after another manner."

Kether, the indivisible unity, reflects Itself into the second sephirah, Chokmah, which is assigned to the zodiac. Thus, the Primal Will of the Crown vitalizes the all-pervasive Life force, known in Hebrew as Chaiah. The Divine Father, Chokmah, then impregnates the Divine Mother, Binah. Here, the saturn principle of contraction and limitation, assigned to this sephirah, begins the manifestation of time and space activating the divine substance. This completes the establishment of the Supernal or Divine Triad (Figure Four). This Triad is the source or the basis of every law, feeling, and thought that eventually becomes the manifested universe. This Supernal triad reflects Itself downward into the "Triad of the Individuality" comprised of the sephiroth of Chesed, Geburah and Tiphareth.

This second triangle of Sephiroth, known as the "Triangle of the Individuality," is so-called because it has at its apex the sephirah Tiphareth. This aspect of the Tree represents the Solar Logos and the Central Self of all humanity, a sort of "Collective Superconsciousness." The first of the other two angles is assigned to Chesed, which represents the cosmic principles of Memory and Mercy. This is a reflection of the supernal sephirah Chokmah, representing the paternal life force and wisdom. The remaining angle reflects the Understanding and form-generating aspects of Binah into Geburah's activity of volition, purpose and law. The triangle of the Individuality is represented as a mirror image of the Supernal triangle. This is to illustrate that our true essential Self is a perfect reflection of the higher spiritual powers. Tiphareth is also considered to be the recipient of these energies, before passing them on to the lower sephiroth.

The next triangle is termed the "Triad of Personality". It shares Tiphareth at its apex with the "Triad of Individuality." This third triangle is made up of Tiphareth, Netzach and Hod. Here is the level where our personality derives its sense of personal identity and separation. Here we observe the development of the intellect in Hod and the emotional nature in Netzach.

These two triads, each with Tiphareth serving as its focusing apex, together form the double triangles of the "Star of David," the beloved. This is the star of the Greater Mysteries.

Tiphareth, the center of our true Self is assigned the Qabalistic title of the "Mediating Intelligence." It is our cosmic destiny to become conscious co-creators of the Universe.

This will be accomplished through the omnipotent power of Love.

Tiphareth receives all of the energies from above its own level and mediates and directs them to all of the sephiroth below it. That is, except to Malkuth, the Kingdom. This sephirah has its foundation in Yesod.

The final triad is composed of Netzach, Hod and Yesod which together include the Desire Nature, the Intellect and the Vital Soul. This is the called "Lower Mental" or "Astral" triad.

Yesod is our gateway to the so-called "Astral Plane." As long as human consciousness is dominated by this triad -- with Hod and Netzach focused upon Yesod -- the initiate's awareness will be under the influence of the distortions and illusions of the accumulated errors in its shared experiences with the Collective Vital Soul called "Nephesh" in Qabalah. A large part of the Path of Initiation involves shifting and then stabilizing our Self-identity from the orientation illustrated by this triangle to that of the triangle whose focus is Tiphareth. While our consciousness is still under the domination of the "house of illusions" that Yesod can be, manifestations in the world of form will mirror these errors. It is the job of the initiate to identify these distortions and lies by careful observation. He must break them up and rebuild them closer to the illuminated patterns of Tiphareth. "Solve et Coagula," "dissolve and reform," advise the alchemists. The initiate polishes and cleanses his "Mirror of the Moon" in Yesod so that it truly reflects the "sunlight" of Tiphareth into our Kingdom.

The Seven Levels of Experience

One of the patterns on the Tree worth examining is the correlation of the sephiroth with the seven levels of experience, (see Table below) and comparing them with the "Seven Stages of Spiritual Awakening" as revealed in the Major Arcana of the Tarot, trumps number 15 through 21. In this study, the applicable Tarot Keys are correlated in reverse order with the seven levels, thus:

Levels	Stage of Awakening	Tarot Key
1	Cosmic Consciousness	21 – The World
2	Realization	20 – Judgment
3	Regeneration	19 – The Sun
4	Reorganization	18 – The Moon
5	Revelation	17 – The Star
6	Awakening	16 – The Tower
7	Bondage	15 – The Devil

The highest principle of the initiate is identical with the "Yekhidah," the "indivisible" which is the Divine Self, the Divine Spark of God. This simultaneously resides on the Spiritual Plane and at the core of every living particle of space. Here is the circle whose center is everywhere and circumference is nowhere. At this stage of experience there is no separation. This is "Cosmic Consciousness." Here, time, space and identity have faded, resulting in the clear realization of beingness. To experience this is to become one with the great "I." As our Eastern brothers express it, it is "perfect peace, transcendence, glory and bliss absolute!" Tarot Key 21, "The World," symbolically depicts this state.

The second level is designated as "The Causal Plane." This plane correlates with the sephiroth Chokmah and Binah on the Tree and is assigned to the second highest aspect of the initiate. Saturn is attributed to Binah. Saturn was the Roman god of time, known in Greece as Chronos. Therefore, it is at this level that we find separation from the indivisible consciousness found in Kether. This is the level of the Divine Life in Chokmah, called "Chaiah" in Hebrew and the Divine Mind, called "Neshamah" in Binah. Key 20, "Judgment," represents these concepts in the Tarot.

Examination of the third level brings us to the "Higher Mental Plane," which is composed of the activities of Chesed and Geburah. Here, the "Individuality" is symbolized by Tiphareth, expressing through the higher functions of Cosmic Memory and Cosmic Purpose, or Will. Tarot Key 19, "The Sun" represents this plane.

The third level is intimately connected with that of the fourth which is called the "Egoic Plane." Here, we see the functioning of Tiphareth as the Central "I," the Ego seated in the hearts of all men. This is the level that marks the initiate as an adept. For here, he becomes aware of the Unity of all Life and his own essential immortality. Key 18, "The Moon," represents the outcome of this revelation.

The fifth level is that of the "Lower Mental Plane." This is the awareness of our normal everyday "waking" consciousness. Also, this is the level of the expression of Divine inspiration as the focus of awareness is turned upward toward Tiphareth, represented by Key 17, "The Star."

The sixth level is that of the "Astral Plane," represented by the functioning of the waking consciousness. However, at this level, it is yielding to the impulses, drives and instincts found at the level of the "Vital Soul" in Yesod. This state is depicted in Tarot as Key 16, "The Tower." This picture represents the destruction of those errors of perception that come about through the insight of illumination that originates at the level of the Individuality. This is enforced by the fact that the "lightning bolt," that knocks down the crown of the false ego originates in the disk of the sun.

The lowest and outermost level of experience is that of the seventh. This is the experience of the "Physical Plane." The awakening to bondage and ignorance is the first requirement in seeking dominion, wisdom and freedom! The sephirah Malkuth as the physical plane is our "magic mirror" whose conditions, appearances and events hold the key to enlightenment and wisdom when they are correctly interpreted as "the effect" and not "the cause." Thus, they direct our attention to the possibility of freedom. This is represented in Key15, "The Devil," by the fact that the loops of the chains around the necks of the man and woman are loose and can be easily removed.

The Triads Major

Qabalists state that the goal of the Great Work is the "reunification of the worlds." This refers to the fact that the initiate can, by centering his consciousness in Tiphareth, become one with the "Mediating Intelligence," and thus bring spirit into conscious physical manifestation.

But how do we learn to center our consciousness at the level of the Ego, the Higher Self? This is the purpose of initiation. We must examine the Greater Triads also known as the "Triads Major" for insights on how to accomplish this, (Figure Four)

The higher of the Triads Major is composed of the sephiroth called Chokmah, Binah and Tiphareth. This triad represents our Individuality coming into full conscious unity with the Divine Wisdom and Understanding. The Ego thus becomes a channel for the Life and Substance of the Source.

The second or lower of these greater triads is composed of Netzach, Hod and Malkuth. This represents the realization that the physical body is an expression of its mental and emotional faculties. It is the vehicle for the expression of the related upper triad. This is pointed out by the fact that both triads are identical in size, proportion and orientation. This indicates to the initiated observer that there is a corresponding relationship between them.

Tiphareth and Malkuth function as the apexes of these two triads, although they are represented at a lower level on the diagram. In addition, the physical body is shown to have some equivalency to the Central Ego, within its own triad, because of the similar orientation of these two sephiroth. This implies that it is through our incarnate experiences that our intellectual and emotional patterns are prepared for the expression of the higher consciousness. We may go to the allegorical "mountain top" of mystical experience, but until we can express these realizations, these patterns of perfection as we negotiate the conflicts, interchanges and apparent lack of harmony in the "marketplace," these mystical insights are not ours! It is easy to love the lovable! Can we love those who are unlovable? This is the true test. We cannot experience and express the higher fulfillment until we express and experience it in the triad of the laboratory of day-to-day life.

The Three Orders and the Grades of Initiation

Finally, we can examine how the grades of initiation fit on the Tree (see Figure Four). We can see that there are, in fact, three "Orders" of Initiation. The first, comprising the sephiroth from Malkuth to Netzach inclusive is sometimes referred to, as we have previously mentioned, as "The Lesser Mysteries." The second is concerned with the sephiroth Tiphareth, Geburah and Chesed. This is called the "Greater Mysteries" or the "Order of Adepts." Finally we have the Third Order, known as the "Supreme Mysteries."

The grades are ten in number, with the addition of the 0=0 grade of Neophyte, which introduces an initiate into the Lesser Mysteries and an unnumbered grade of "Portal" which fulfills a similar function for the Greater Mysteries. The grades are designated by titles in Latin and a set of two numbers connected by an "equal" sign. The first set of numbers refer to the sequential number of the grade while the second set refers to the sephirah that the particular grade is attributed to on the Tree of Life.

The traditional grades are as follows:

First Order:
    1=10   Zelator
    2=9   Theoricus
    3=8   Practicus
    4=7   Philosophus

Second Order:
    5=6   Adeptus Minor
    6=5   Adeptus Major
    7=4   Adeptus Exemptus

Third Order:
    8=3   Magister Templi
    9=2   Magus
    10=1   Ipsissimus

Although these grade names were made famous by the historical "Hermetic Order of the Golden Dawn," they did not originate with this order nor with their predecessors of the S:.R:.I:.A:. Both merely adopted these designations for their use.

Chapter 18
Except the Lord Build the House

"All Paths that lead to God are good." This assertion made here is irrefutable! It may, however, raise the ire of many who have been conditioned by dogma and early childhood indoctrination to think that there is only one way to the Divine. Some of these individuals like to play what I call the "My God is bigger than your God," game.

Jesus said "I am the way, the truth and the life and no one comes to the Father but by (or through) me." The prophet Muhammad, on the other hand is reported to have observed, "The ways to God are as numerous as the breaths of the Sons of Man." How are these various statements reconciled? Is one true while the other is false?

There is but One Spirit through which we might reach union with the Divine. But that Spirit is resident within each one of us. It exists at that point where our soul lies open to the Infinite. As Jesus said, "The Kingdom of Heaven is within." And again, "Seek ye first the Kingdom..." All systems, exercises, ceremonies or teachers are only worthwhile if they facilitate this experience. This goal is referred to in the Mysteries as "illumination" or "the Greater Initiation." It is a physiological, psychological and spiritual phenomenon. It is the subject of true Spiritual Alchemy, Yoga, Qabalah, Tantra and Magic. As a result of this experience the initiate becomes consciously immortal. It is no longer a matter of faith or belief; it is *Gnosis* or certain knowledge. It is more than the attainment of Wisdom, it is the embodiment of this much sought after quality.

This experience allows the Individuality to directly express through the personality. It is to facilitate this transformation and dedicate the resultant higher consciousness to the service of humanity that the initiatory schools were founded. This is still the purpose of the esoteric orders today. The preparation of the personality/body vehicles is the province of the Lesser Mysteries. The awakening of this higher perception and its subsequent use is what concerns the Greater Mysteries.

This preparation must occur in a balanced way. The natural personality, built up in the ordinary course of an incarnation, is formed, as we have pointed out, in response to the environment and the relationships our life experiences offer to us. It may or may not be efficiently designed to deal with the forces of the world, but it certainly is ill equipped to handle the high-tension currents encountered by the adept. This is the reason that Qabalah, Mysticism, and the Occult are criticized as dangerous, on the one hand, and the province of the mentally unbalanced on the other.

Many have ill-adapted psychological mechanisms when they first approach the occult disciplines. If these are not corrected by a balanced development and method, the inadequacies will act as a fault line that may fracture. Thus are produced the well-known phenomenon of the "crack-pot!"

The sacred energy manifests in three basic ways which human consciousness perceives as *Omnipotence* - all power, *Omniscience* - all knowing, and, *Omnipresence* - present everywhere. These are sometimes simply referred to as the rays of Power, Wisdom, and Love.

It will be noted by those readers who have studied the Eastern Path that these classifications are approximately equivalent to those presented in the *Bhagavad Gita*. There they are called *Raja* – power, *Gnani* – wisdom and *Bhakti* – love or devotion. The human constitution as well as the Cosmos are naturally comprised of these three components. In the East, they are referred to as the "Gunas." All energy, all consciousness, all manifestation is naturally organized or related to these three expressions. There is an initiating expression (Power); a stabilizing expression (Love); and, an expression that mediates or balances between the two (Wisdom). This is shown on the Tree by the three pillars and appears in other depictions.

A balance of these three aspects is always essential. Power and Wisdom untempered by Love leads to a dangerous combination where the esoteric knowledge becomes devoid of a conscience and the vital dedication to serve the Light. Power and Love without the guidance of Wisdom becomes unrestricted passion, revealing also that even the best of intentions may go awry if not tempered by experience. Wisdom and Love mated without Power becomes ineffectual sentimentality. All three in combination are truly the royal qualities of the enlightened initiate. We will examine each of the three paths in the next chapter.

Chapter 19
The Three Paths to Awakening

Traditionally, and in the contemporary Mystery Schools of the West, initiatory linkage to the three paths must be offered as a complete system. These three paths correspond to the three dominant "rays" of the Lesser Mysteries. They are known as the Hermetic or Orange Ray, the Celtic or Green Ray, and the Purple or Orphic Ray. They take their names from the historical schools that best represented the initiation of these qualities.

The Hermetic Ray

The Orange Ray is named after the legendary Egyptian Mage, Hermes Trismegistus. The Egyptian Schools of Thoth, the Qabalah, and later the Alexandrian and Fez schools epitomize this type of initiatory work.

Hermes may have been, like Zoroaster, a hierarchical title, passed from one generation of high priests to another. However, this title has been associated with a specific individual, Melchizedek, whom our tradition tentatively identifies as an Atlantean Adept.

The Orange Ray correlates with the sephirah Hod on the Tree of Life. The path is roughly equivalent to Gnani Yoga in the Eastern Tradition. It is the Way of Wisdom and of the mind. It is a way of study and the science of correspondences.

On this path we find "High Magic" and the "Practical Qabalah." This is the way of hidden knowledge and the occult sciences, not the arts. The ancient Egyptian god "Tehuti," an aspect of Thoth, rules it. The Mysteries of Egypt and the Qabalah are good examples of this approach. Fictional examples can be found in the *Secrets of Dr. Taverner* by Dion Fortune, and my own book, *The Broken Seal and Other Cases*.

The Celtic Ray

The Celtic Ray represents an approach to the hidden light via the forces of nature. Good fictional examples can be found in the works of Arthur Machen, Algernon Blackwood and in Dion Fortune's *Goat Foot God* and *Sea Priestess*.

It is the Celtic Ray, also called the "Green Ray," that gives the initiate vitality and a zest for life. Without it the aspirant tends to become overly intellectual and prone to being a mere theorist. Dion Fortune states that this ray correlates with the "Upper Astral Plane."

This is the Way of the Artist. It feeds creative artistic expression. Where the Hermetic Ray has for its beacon Truth, the Green Ray's ideal is Beauty.

Initiates work upon the Power Principle on this path.

The Orphic Ray

The Orphic or Purple Ray is also known as the Christian Ray or the Way of the Grail. It is the path of the Devotional Mystic, the "Way of the Heart."

It is very much an inward path. On it, one may contact and know the all-embracing, unconditional love of God. The initiate's task on this path is to transmit the healing of this love to all who call to the Lord of the Universe for aid.

Some Mystics have noted a feeling of profound sadness at various times on this path. It is not a symptom of depression but rather the manifestation of the initiate's capacity to sense and be one with the very real suffering of much of humanity. Even though the aspirant feels the sadness, it is also an occasion for great joy! By this "oneness" with the soul of humanity they can, in a very real sense, transmute this suffering. They can realize that they have the power to bless this collective soul while the feeling flows through them and to consciously aid in the healing of it. Since they have realized the creative power of consciousness, they may counteract the lies that are at the root of this pain. They "light one candle," a light that all the darkness in the Universe cannot overcome! They become the Grail, pouring out healing and harmony and thereby healing all the land.

These three rays get their names from the three sephiroth that immediately lead to the inner from Malkuth: Orange for Hod and the Ray of Wisdom, Green for Netzach and the Ray of Power, and Purple for Yesod and the Ray of Love. They each have a higher corollary in the Greater Mysteries: the Blue of Chesed as the higher octave of the Wisdom Ray, the Red of Geburah for the Power Ray, and finally, the Yellow of Tiphareth for the Ray of the Grail and the Love of God.

PART THREE

The Method of the Mysteries

Chapter 20
Within the Portal

What causes the changes that transform an initiate from Neophyte to Adept? What are these changes? In brief, what exactly is the "Method of the Mysteries?"

It is said, "By their fruit shall you know them" (Matthew 7:16). And the Mysteries of the esoteric tradition can point with pride to many just men and women made perfect. But the system is not always perfect and some of the initiates do not emerge from the Vault of Initiation truly transmuted into the "Stone of the Wise." What is the difference that enables some to succeed and others to flounder?

Hermes Trismegistus said, "Equilibrium is the secret of the Great Work." Many allow themselves to be drawn to extremes. Nowhere is this truer than in the Mysteries. Some seekers feel that only by extreme measures, departing from everyday realities, can we succeed on the Path. Nothing could be farther from the truth. The title of Crank, Follower of Fads, or Crackpot do not characterize the adept! Thus, balance and a step-by-step process of unfoldment is key to the successful fulfillment of the work. Patterns of balance have always been part of the true Mysteries.

The central symbol of the Mysteries of the West is the Tree of Life. This Tree is conceived of as having its roots in heaven and its branches linking the way from the manifest to the spiritual. It correlates with Jacob's Ladder and the Spindle of the World. We find this symbol in the *Tuat* of the Egyptians and the *Ygsidril* of the Vikings. But undoubtedly, the most developed of these tree symbols is found in the Qabalistic Tree of Life. This symbol is well known to students of esoteric teachings.

The Tree of Life provides a systematic theoretical framework for transforming consciousness as is taught in the Arcane Orders. In this section, we will explore the grades as they are taught in the esoteric fraternities. We will first look at that part of the Tree that is assigned to the personality. This is, as has been pointed out previously, that section referred to as "The Lesser Mysteries." Next we will consider the change in consciousness that must occur to awaken the fire of Adepthood within the being of the initiate. Finally, we will discuss the work of "The Greater Mysteries".

Chapter 21
The Initiation of Earth

Earth, the material or the physical plane refer to the "adversary" in most outer forms of spiritual development. The manifest world is seen as something that has entrapped the soul, entangling it in bondage to matter. It is viewed in these schools as something from which to escape. Yet, in the esoteric initiatory fraternity of the Western Tradition in which I received my training, this so-called snare of illusion is the first step on the journey to adeptship.

In the Qabalah, the tenth sephirah is called Malkuth and is assigned to Earth. Macrocosmically this refers to the physical universe, the "luminous garment of Adonai." Microcosmically its counterpart is the human body, the so-called "harp of ten thousand strings." This sephirah, viewed as the fruit of the Tree of Life, is the miracle of God's creation. It is also thought of as the great magic mirror for the expression of our personal thought patterns.

In the ancient Qabalistic text, *The 32 Paths of Wisdom,* Malkuth is described as follows:

> *The Tenth Path is called the Resplendent Intelligence because it is exalted above every head and sits upon the Throne of Binah (Understanding). It illumines the splendors of all the lights, and causes the holy influence (Mezla) to descend from the Prince of Countenances (Metatron), the angel of Kether.*

Thus, in this passage we are informed that manifestation is the purpose of creation! Microcosmically, this was expressed in a statement received by Paul Foster Case, "The Kingdom of Spirit is embodied in my flesh." (*The Pattern on the Trestleboard*)

The Initiation of Earth involves as whole new way of looking at the manifested universe, a whole new point of view as to our purpose as conscious entities functioning in it.

The psychological effect of these "elemental attunements" can be dramatic. I remember my teacher, who had been raised in Brooklyn, New York, and had always lived in cities of concrete and asphalt, told me a story connected with this. She had just gone through her Earth Initiation and in the weeks that followed she became passionate for gardening. She, of course, was totally inexperienced in the subject, but she felt compelled to get her hands in the dirt and bring forth living things! She selected a patch, approximately five feet square, pulled all the grass up and planted her crop of vegetables! She couldn't understand why all the other initiates were quite amused at her behavior until she recognized the connection between her attunement to the earth grade and her new career as a "farmer!"

In the Fraternity of the Hidden Light, as with most of the initiatory schools of the West, we encourage our members to renew or reconfirm their contact with the consciousness of the Earth. They are asked to get away from the concrete jungles of city existence, if only for a day or two, now and then, and to walk and experience the blessings and awareness of the Divine in Nature. This re-sourcing regularly produces dramatic, "magical" benefits of a renewed life with vitality and balance.

Aleister Crowley climbed mountains. S.L. Macgregor Mathers boxed. Many of my fraters and sorors exercise, do Hatha Yoga or are involved in one of the martial arts. The need for a vigorous "earthing" activity is necessary to maintain balance. Initiates of the Western Mysteries do not run away from the manifest world but seek rather to spiritualize their awareness of it.

In this grade, special attention is paid to basic nutrition. We are instructed to eat a wide variety of foods for one can never know which combination of nutrients might become critical in the Great Work, as each one of us is unique. We are encouraged to eat fresh foods as often as practicable. Eat what we like and what agrees with us, but eat only half of what we can comfortably hold! Avoid becoming a faddist or fanatic. The mindset of a "crank" effectively prevents the higher awakening. Eat with reverence, visualizing Life's energy in every bite. Through our visualizations we come to realize that we are eating will become "illumination material."

Drink plenty of water for the "inner alchemist" of our subconsciousness must have liquids to facilitate the magic potions of our glands. Get enough sunlight, but not to the extent of risking melanoma! Get fresh air and breathe it properly, with deep inhalations from the diaphragm, breathing through the nose.

In the grade of Earth we are introduced to the subject of Alchemy. The reader is cautioned that, for the initiate, this subject bears little resemblance to what they are probably familiar with from uninitiated authors. This work is concerned with the physical reconstruction of the body. We strengthen and purify our bodies through correct habits of diet, breathing and exercise. It is through attention to this "gross work" that the foundations are laid for the more advanced work.

Special instruction is given on the subject of directing the subtle energies known as the

Etheric. Practices for controlling currents of energy by "banishing" and "invoking" are studied.

The realization of the sacredness of the Earth and the fact that God's consciousness is experiencing His/Her miracle through us is exemplified in the words attributed to Chief Seattle, "Man did not weave the web of life – he is merely a strand in it. Whatever he does to the web, he does to himself." The "web of life" describes an interrelated unity of conscious awareness. The initiate knows that there is no such thing as "dead matter." They <u>know</u> that the One Consciousness slumbers in the mineral, dreams in the plant, awakens in the animal and becomes aware in the human. It is for those who have awakened to the next stage to herald the truth that it is the Divine in Whom we live and move and have our being.

Chapter 22
The All is Mind

The ALL as the "Substantial Reality underlying all the outward manifestations and appearances which we know under the terms of The Material Universe...is SPIRIT, which in itself is Unknowable and Undefinable, but which may be considered and thought of as an Universal, Infinite, Living Mind. (The Kybalion, p.26)

God is often described as being both immanent and transcendent. That is, the Divine Consciousness is intensely present in every atom, every particle of manifestation, at every stage of the process. This is immanence. But God is also transcendent – or put another way there is more to God than just our collection of universes.

Hermeticism affirms that the universe is primarily a creation of Divine Mind. As far as this space/time continuum is concerned, there is nothing else but Divine Consciousness, however that consciousness decides to manifest or represent Itself.

But if this is so, upon what does this Consciousness operate, through what does it act? Out of what is the Universe created? To answer, "the Void," or "the Nothingness," is to merely draw a curtain across the stage of Genesis and state that it is unknowable. And while it is true that human consciousness is not equipped, at least at the present stage of its evolution, to comprehend the root of creation, we must consider the implications of these questions for the theory of "the way of initiation."

If we follow the thread of concepts that we have inherited from the ancient Hermeticists, we learn that, "The All is Mind, the Universe is Mental." (*The Kybalion*) Everything that ever was, is or will be, in all of its infinite variations exists within the mind of God. How could it be otherwise? Outside of God, The All, "in whom we live and move and have our being," there is naught. If something or someone has an existence separate or outside of The All, the "The All" is misnamed; it is only "the Part!"

The Hermetic Law of Correspondence states: "As Above, so Below, as Below, so Above, for the performance of the miracles of the One Thing." What does this really mean to us?

First, we must remember that the "Above" or heaven was conceived as the place of the beginnings or causes, "…may Thy will be done on Earth as it is in Heaven…" The "Above" is the place of the Divine, eternal Will or purpose. The "Below" or Earth is the effect, and often times the method by which we judge the success of our operation. Modern metaphysicians often substitute the word "Within" for the above in this law. This is done to emphasize the immanence of the creative power.

The important point in connection with this discussion is that Cause is always internal. It proceeds from that point of Divine connection, that center of omnipotence, omniscience and omnipresence that constitutes the One Reality in each one of us. Never, I repeat, never does anything outside of ourselves occurring in the world of effects cause us to feel, act or be anything. These are matters of choice, of Free Will. That will is free to the extent, and only to the extent, that it is identified or aligned with The One Will — for only then will it reflect reality.

The ancient sages called consciousness "The First Matter" and described three modes of expression. They said it acted:

[1] To hold or preserve;
[2] To excite and transform;
[3] To flow or equilibrate and
    take form.

The Alchemists symbolized these three by the symbols (1) ⊖ - Salt, (2) ⚢ - Sulphur, (3) ☿ - Mercury. These are identical to the three "Gunas" of Yoga philosophy which calls them: [1] Tamas; [2] Rajas; [3] Satva.

Most modern "depth" schools of psychology also define three modes of expression or functioning of consciousness. Naturally they define these by how they function in relation to human consciousness. We have a "self-conscious" mode. This is our waking mind. It observes and establishes premises which are passed along to the next mode of mind which is variously called the "Unconscious, Subconscious, or Deep Consciousness." This is the mode that is concerned with memory, autonomic nervous functions (i.e. digestion, respiration, body chemistry, etc.) as well as the dream state. The Subconscious and Self-conscious modes comprise, to a large extent, what we know as the Personality.

The third mode is called "The Superconscious, Higher Self, The True Self, The Christ Self" not only encompasses the other two, but is more. It is our immediate Divine link. It is often referred to as simply "The Individuality." In the mystic literature it is said that: "The Personality is the vehicle of consciousness for an incarnation, but it is the Individuality that is the vehicle for an evolution."

It is a mistake, however, to think of these modes of consciousness as actual separations or divisions in our mind. They are the ways that the ONE MIND functions through us. As Dr. Ernest Homes, the founder of Religious Science, writes in his Science of Mind (1926) Textbook, "When a man uses his mind he is, at the same time, using the Great Mind." He is in agreement with the ancient sages in this statement. It points out that the appearance of an individual mind is an illusion. When a person is utilizing his mind he is functioning as a channel for the Universal Creative Consciousness. This "frees" us from the mistaken concept that we are, in any way, limited in our power to create through consciousness. We are centers of expression for the same Will, Creativity, Mind and Love that brought the Universe into being and is continually creating and sustaining it.

When the Mind of the Creator "hovered" or "brooded" upon the face of the Deep, it was an act of creative imaging! Everything that ever was, is or will be is an outcome of this activity of mind. This is the same Great Mind that flows through us at every moment. The person who complains that they cannot concentrate, that they lack will power, that they are unable to achieve their goals, or that they are uninspired develops self-fulfilling and unfulfilling prophesies. They strangle the manifestation of the beauty of the Divine expression flowing through them and give form to the state of lack they are complaining about.

In the Mind of God we "live and move and have our being." The entire creation of everything was and is an act of the Divine Imagination. Many have come to equate the imagination with the "unreal." This is a symptom of one of the Lies of Separation. This part of the Lie states simply that the so-called objective world is the basis, the standard for reality. That the subjective states of consciousness are only relevant to the extent that they confirm the outside experience. Actually the opposite is closer to the truth. As we previously mentioned, Causation is always internal. For it is the purpose of our imagination to provide the matrix for future manifestation. We will discuss this further.

The fact that the One Mind lives through us answers one of the Cardinal Questions, "Why were we created?" The answer is that the One Mind created us to experience Itself through an infinite number of unique viewpoints. Some will object that the One Self already is omniscient. I would submit that God certainly is aware of HIS/HER own perfection. Wholeness is, in fact, omniscient. But this wholeness is an evolving perfection and it is on a cosmic scale. We were created so that He could experience Her creation from an infinite variety of unique viewpoints. Let me illustrate this with a true story.

One of the great shortcomings of many schools of mystical philosophy is that they tend to fall into the trap of dualism. For them Spirit and Matter seem to be two irreconcilable opposites. They emphasize Spirit as desirable, relegating the manifest as an illusionary distraction that must be overcome as soon as possible.

The Qabalists, on the other hand, view the material universe as the flower of the Tree of

Life. It is the "out picturing" or expression of the inner spiritual truth. Jesus referred to this analogy when he stated, "by their fruit ye shall know them."

During the period of time that I was in my early teens through my late twenties, I was trained in spiritual transformative disciplines in association with a certain esoteric school. My primary teacher was an exceptionally gifted mystic who was an expert in the Hermetic Qabalah.

My teacher accepted the doctrine that God experiences His creation through us, and therefore attempted in every way to "spiritualize" each mundane activity she encountered in her daily experience. Once, for example, a group of us accompanied her to the legendary Chronicle Restaurant in Pasadena, California. About a dozen of us were seated at a large round table smack in the middle of the dining room. When it came time for dessert, we ordered a wide selection.

Now the Chronicle was well known for its outstanding desserts and when our teacher was served, she literally "meditated" her portion. She inhaled the fragrance, savored the texture, and relished the flavor! She went into ecstasy, oohing and ahhing at each bite. Then, she offered each of us a bite and encouraged us to do the same. Afterwards we passed around samples of our own desserts as well!

I will admit that we, but not our teacher, were somewhat self-conscious about all the fuss we made of eating! Everyone was watching us. Then we noticed that two very conservatively dressed businessmen in three piece suits were watching us especially closely. When they got up from their table and approached us, we did not know what to expect. They apologized for interrupting our meal, but admitted that they had been observing us, and, frankly stated that they had never ever seen anyone enjoy their meal as much as our teacher.

She explained to them that she was our spiritual mentor and had been modeling a spiritual discipline for us. She started to apologize if our activity had disturbed their meal or conversation when the gentlemen stopped her, saying, "No, no we think it is wonderful! You see," they continued, "we are the owners of this restaurant and we cannot think of a better advertisement than watching you enjoy your meal. We want you to know," they finished, "that if you will provide us with just 30 minutes advance notice of when you are planning to dine with us, that this table will always be reserved for you!"

She was teaching us through her example the esoteric principle that God experiences His creation through us. Each of us has a unique viewpoint for experiencing and evolving and each is necessary to experience the Whole. This is the way we give back to the Infinite Supply, the Universal Consciousness, and The Great Mind.

Chapter 23
Consciousness Creates

There were once two monks. One was young and was struggling to learn about the way of enlightenment and to find his real identity. He was assigned to travel with an aged monk who was to act as his mentor, teaching the younger man through precept and example the meaning of Life and the Way of Unfoldment.

One day, the old Sage asked his young protégé to fetch some herbs from his pack so that he might prepare a medicine for an ill person that they had been asked to help. As the young monk was searching through his mentor's possessions for the herbs, he happened to find a hand-mirror at the bottom of the pack. This caused him to wonder in agitation. Why did his teacher have this article in his possession? Did the old man still have a problem with vanity? Did he "sneak" a look at his reflection when nobody was looking? The more time that passed, the more obsessed he became with his conjectures, until he could no longer contain it.

At the close of an autumn day of travel, as they were eating their meal of rice around the dying embers of the campfire, the young man could hold his silence no longer. "Venerable Sir! Why do you carry a hand mirror with you?"

The Old Man looked surprised, and then, having divined the intent of his protégé's question, chuckled. He opened his pack, retrieved the mirror and passed it to the young man and motioned him to look at his reflection gazing back at him.

"I carry that looking glass with me so that, whenever the troubles of the Path beset me, as they must to us all; whenever the challenges of Life come up hard against me, I may look into it and see the image of the one responsible for my woes. There also, at the same moment, I see the source of the solution of all my problems. Indeed, I seek not to change the world but rather myself and thus alter my world!"

The "double-sided" coin, incorporating both responsibility and power, seems to be, to a large extent, out of fashion in our postmodern society. From frivolous lawsuits to "the Devil made me do it," patterns of blaming others have reached epidemic proportions. Each time we blame another we give up a bit of our divinely gifted power. We become vulnerable to "the effect" of people, conditions and events.

But initiates of the mystery schools and those that are just "more aware" have uniformly affirmed the principle of inner causation. This principle states that, contrary to appearances, never does anything outside of ourselves cause us to do, be or experience anything. The point of power, of causation, exists within.

Victor Frankl, one of the greatest psychiatrists of the twentieth century, wrote in his book, *Man's Search for Meaning*, of his experience of internment in the Nazi concentration camps during the Second World War. He tells us of his recollection of a muddy winter day when he and hundreds of others were being herded through the gates into the depths of Auschwitz. He rushed up to the sergeant in charge of the gate and held out a package containing hundreds of pages of his paper, the result of decades of research that he had conducted on the treatment of the mentally ill. He explained to the guard that it didn't matter what happened to him, but that his work, represented in the thick stock of papers he was urging the soldier to take, was most important to the people of Germany.

The guard took the papers nodding and answered, "Yah, Yah!" He then, to Dr. Frankl's dismay, flung the papers onto the ground and forced Victor to watch as hundreds of feet of his fellow captives trod upon them into the mud.

Rather than reacting to this and the constant efforts at dehumanization that he experienced, he chose his response. Dr. Frankl seemed to hear a small voice from within that told him that he was still in control. No matter how his jailers attempted to degrade, humiliate or control him, he still had a choice. In that split second between his oppressors' stimulus and his response there was always, within him, that point of choice, that causative nexus where he had the power to choose his reaction and thus control his future. True, the Nazis could have killed him, could restrict his liberty, but they could not restrict his freedom to choose how he faced that event.

This was demonstrated to him repeatedly in the day-to-day horror of life in the camp. According to the philosophy of his jailers, the deprivation of food, water, clothing and rest should have forced the internees to degenerate to the level of primitives. They predicted that when people were forced to this level by influence beyond their control they would revert to a "survival of the fittest" mentality. What they were to see, however, were people reaching out to help each other, individuals giving up their food or blanket to help a weaker or sick fellow inmate. Try as they might, the Nazis could not defeat the spirit of their prisoners. Why? Because the power of choice resides within and at that nexus resides the power to create our own reality.

The outer world, falsely considered to be the world of causation, should serve to act as our "magic mirror." Here we may determine the state of our inner universe. If we perceive hate, strife or turbulence impinging upon us, we need to look inward to our consciousness to correct the situation.

Consciousness creates! We indeed are made in the image and likeness of the Creator. Not necessarily in a physical sense, but in terms of consciousness. We are centers of expression of the same power that creates and sustains the sun and the planets. Indeed, we create our universe on a moment-to-moment basis according to the images we choose to habitually hold in our consciousness and energize with our desire force. Within us is the power. And with great power comes great responsibility.

A friend of mine cautioned me to not emphasize the big "R" word. He reflected that I might scare potential readers before the first chapter. I answered that while that might be a possibility with some segments of the public, I felt it was unlikely with individuals who would be interested in this book. I further explained that the readership of this book is not only likely to take responsibility for their actions but also for the attainment of their goals. They were, most probably, not materialistic and thus were open to the possibility of an inward source of power and would be motivated by a higher vision. Also, the vast majority of these "self-actualizing" seekers would be motivated by a strong sense of purpose to achieve their full potential so that they, in turn, could better serve others. Their motive for service is indeed the only safe way to awaken and develop the skills and powers of the path of initiation.

A wise man once observed, "I am a spiritual being having a human experience, not a human being having a spiritual experience." Who or what are we? Ancient Wisdom asserts that the personality/body complex, as miraculous as it is, is far from being all there is to us. At the center of our being, exists a point of conscious awareness that is, in every sense, identical with the One Perfection that is the source, vehicle and manifestation of complete

Power, Wisdom and Love. This point of awareness is beyond and through eternity. It is beyond and through all space. It is all consciousness. It is Divine and it is in each one of us, undivided, one, whole. And it is affirmed that, if it is in each one of us and it is One – then we are in union, there is only one of us! That One is on a Grand Quest, a journey from a state of unconscious unity through a state of conscious awareness of the many, to finally arrive at perfect Cosmic Consciousness. It is this journey, this process that we are all concerned with. We are concerned with this marvelous game of the evolution of consciousness. What are the rules? What is the playing field? Who are our teammates?

The importance of these questions becomes clear to the initiate when he or she has reached a sufficiently awakened state of consciousness. Even at the very beginning, there is the realization that in order to achieve our full potential, in order to fulfill our destiny, we must take an active role. We must become co-creators in the Great Work of Transformation of – us! Only by this will we come, at length, to enjoy our highest good.

When the "Serpent of Wisdom" tempted the soul to eat of the forbidden fruit of the Tree of Knowledge of Good and Evil, humankind became aware of all of the pairs of opposites. With this awareness of differences came the conscious level of thought. It was, in fact, an evolutionary step. We became "homo-sapiens" thinking or knowing kind. This was the departure point for the Great Quest. The so-called "fall from grace" was actually part of the Divine plan. God expected, had calculated for it, just as parents today expect their teenagers to try their wings of independence at a certain stage of their development. Humankind was not driven from the state of consciousness symbolized by the Garden of Eden as much as we graduated to another level.

Chapter 24
The Principle of Attention

Attention gives life. What we focus our attention upon and energize with our emotions, our desire power, is planted, nurtured and watered in the garden of our consciousness. This is the power of our Conscious mode of mind.

The water analogy is apt. When we concentrate, we focus units of attention upon a certain image or idea. It then springs to life, just as when we water the plants in our garden. Our waking consciousness plants the seeds and supplies the water. Jesus tells the story of a farmer who found that an enemy had stolen into his fields by night and had sown tares (or weeds) in with his wheat.

Another parable put he forth unto them, saying. The Kingdom of heaven is likened unto a man, which sowed good seed in his field. But while men slept, his enemy came and sowed tares among the wheat, and went his way. But when the wheat was sprung up, and brought forth first, then appeared tares also. So the servants of the householder came and said unto him. Sir, didst not thou sow good seed in thy field? From whence then hath it tares? He said unto them, An enemy hath done this. The servants said unto him, Wilt thou then we go and gather them up? But he said, Nay; lest while ye gather up the tares, ye root up also the wheat with them. Let both grow together until the harvest: and in the time of harvest I will say unto the reapers, Gather ye together first the tares and bind them in bundles to burn them: but gather the wheat into my barn. (Matthew 13:34-30)

A metaphysical interpretation of this parable will help us to understand a few important points about the principle of attention.

The field symbolizes our deep consciousness, usually referred to as the subconscious mind. We will discuss this mode of consciousness in the chapter "How Consciousness Creates." Here, it is enough to point out that this activity of mind can be likened to a garden or, as we have pointed out, a field. It reproduces states and suggestions implanted there from the conscious level and "out pictures" or expresses them as actual conditions or events in the manifest. Thus, into this field of subconscious activities the "good" wheat is sown. "What we sow, so shall we reap," right? How do we, therefore, explain the tares and weeds?

The wheat represents our positive, Christ-centered, evolutionary thoughts, reflecting our Individuality. Thoughts that are based upon our higher understanding of the true nature of God, the Universe and ourselves. But we are not an island unto ourselves. Although we share, through our deep consciousness, the thoughts of the saints and avatars of all time, we also share the errors of the race consciousness, both present and past. These are the errors based upon the great lies of Materialism, Mortality, and Separation. The "tares" such as "what you see is the whole truth," "when you're dead you're dead," and, "do unto others before they do it unto you," have over the centuries permeated the mass mind consciousness. They are reflected in our educational system, our sports, entertainment activities, economics, and even in our religions. Their subtle implications are responsible for the majority of fear, misery, anger and grief that we encounter in the world today. Even a vigilant consciousness will see some of these "tares" cropping up in his or her field of consciousness. Yet the parable points out that we may not "root-out" these errors by going into the subconsciousness. This is not only impracticable, but also dangerous. Which of our intellects is up to the task of performing the jobs that even an infant's subconscious mind does on a routine basis?

I remember one case reported to me where a student of Hatha Yoga (that branch of yoga that deals with the physical body) concentrated assiduously for many weeks on gaining conscious control over his autonomic functions. He finally succeeded in transferring command of his breathing from the subconscious to the conscious level of his mind. Then the student spent three days of sleeplessness anxiously trying to convince the subconsciousness to take control of the breath once more! Imagine the problem if it had been his heartbeat instead!

No, as the parable advises us, the proper way to eliminate these negative patterns, these "weeds" from our consciousness is to observe their appearance at the harvest, once it reaches manifestation. Then we can separate the wheat from the tares by utilizing the transformative power of our desire force. This power, symbolized by fire, the transforming element, in the parable is controlled by our attention. We reinforce and reproduce the patterns we pay attention to and energize.

Almost everyone knows the story of the newlyweds. When they were first married, they could not bear to be apart. Each day brought a new treasure in their relationship. Then, about one year later, according to the story, the bride noticed whiskers left in the lavatory and her husband sometimes left the seat up. He crumbled his crackers into his soup, etc. The husband, on the other hand, noticed that his wife left newly washed underwear hanging in the shower. She squeezed the toothpaste from the top of the tube and sometimes, she even placed the toilet paper the wrong way on the dispenser!

Silly, right? But if they forgot why they fell in love, if they chose to direct their attention to this two to five percent of imperfection, (instead of focusing on the other 98% of beautiful, lovable characteristics that are perfection) they would grow apart. They would find that these shortcomings assume a larger and larger degree of importance, all out of proportion with reality. Like weeds in a garden, if we water them, they will grow and spread and finally choke out the intended crop. Instead, if we deprive the tares of the water, if we consistently refute what we know to be error and focus instead on the positive, the weeds will die out. Instead, the flowers or wheat will prosper. In our example, the honeymoon may be over but the fire of romance can be rekindled by focusing on the lovable characteristics of the beloved.

One point. When we notice an error in our creations, it is important to not reject them with a great deal of vehemence. Instead, gently, firmly and lovingly; simply switch our attention or focus – our point of concentration – from the negative pattern to the positive, fulfilling one. Remember, attention gives life. We are starving the negative thought, image or behavior, not beating it into submission. When we energize our shift of focus by vehemently rejecting the unwanted pattern, it sends a suggestion, a seed to our subconsciousness, that it must be hard work, requiring an iron will and a great deal of effort to shift our focus and de-energize the old image.

Chapter 25
The Initiation of Air

Initiation is a process. It is not a product, but a journey. I am inviting you to participate in the process. There is no dogma or doctrine that is a substitute for inner experiences. In the grade of Air we are given the road map of this journey.

Remember, nothing outside of one's self is magical, unless it is found also within, at our center of centers. True creativity is the ability to get beyond one's self-imposed limitations.

In the grade of Earth we are shown how to intensify our aspiration. Initiates are taught the vital importance of desire and zeal. Indeed, an earnest aspiration is a prerequisite for arousing the energy needed to begin the journey of awakening.

In the grade of Air, the area of activity is shifted from the body to the activities of the psychical nature and how we may purify the automatic responses to the stimuli presented to us through our life experience. We seek to become more and more aware of how some of our patterns of response are not in harmony with our aspiration to become transparent vehicles for our Higher Self. It is by repeated acts of conscious attention to correcting and aligning these responses that we direct the awesome power of our deep consciousness to connect with the centers of empowerment known as Archetypes.

The Law of Response states that man has dominion over all levels of consciousness below the self-conscious level. Additionally, subconsciousness is completely and unfailingly responsive to direction from this level. This control must be based upon a foundation of right knowledge that is applied through practices that demonstrate that we are centers of expression for the Universal Mind. We must establish this concept by eliminating feelings, attitudes, habits, and speech patterns that support the lie of limitation and instead reinforce the idea that we have limitless power to accomplish our goals. The truth is that we potentially have within us all the power there is, if we could but liberate it so that our personalities function as instrument of its expression. This liberation is accomplished by conscientiously and persistently practicing the attitude expressed by the old Rosicrucian vow, "I will look upon every circumstance in my life as a <u>direct</u> dealing of God with my soul."

The initiation of Air is attributed to the sephirah Yesod. It carries the title in Latin of "Theoricus" which means, "one who is instructed in theory." Every legitimate western school of initiation requires their members to be well versed in theory before progressing to practice. Without this foundation of knowledge our work degenerates into superstition. We need, however, to realize that practice and theory must go hand-in-hand in a balanced partnership. This is emphasized by the Hebrew title for this grade which is "Baal ha Da'ath" or "Lord or Master of Knowledge." Right knowledge is what prepares us for effective practice, but, important as it is, it simply prepares and aids us in forming our hypothesis. Practice builds knowledge into the response patterns of deep consciousness and thus effects a transmutation of awareness that manifests in our lives.

We must recognize the often-overlooked fact that the level of deep consciousness links us to the errors as well as the great truths of the past. However, this level is always and unfailingly under the control of our self-conscious mind. Therefore, we can transform our reactions to these errors and the influence that they appear to exert on us. We do this by the correct use of the imagination. We can affirmatively redirect the energy that is held in bondage to these patterns, originating in past errors, into new patterns that are more in line with the truth of our higher aspirations. Thus we move from pain to triumph by changing our reactions from established patterns, or paths of least resistance, to new and more evolved responses.

Just as the land owner in the parable of the wheat and tares instructed his field workers to wait until harvest to separate the wheat from the weeds, so we find that we must start this process with a careful, objective analysis of a present situation that seems to restrict and cause us pain. We must see it as the natural outcome of a chain of causation that our ego set in motion in the past. We can then change our future responses in a proactive manner, more in accordance with the goals of our higher aspiration to influence that future. Thus, little by little we find that we are affirmatively and consistently imaging, as far as our present state of comprehension will permit, the new image of illuminated consciousness.

Among the most important errors that must be corrected and rebalanced are those related to the reproductive energy. Many of these images are totally inappropriate for the initiate. The uncleanness or sinfulness, which are so deeply associated with it at the popular level of our society, must be totally purged from the consciousness of the aspirant. No matter how misused it has been, we have to realize that it is sacred. It is this inner sacred energy that is directed to awaken the dormant centers of spiritual illumination. This new direction of the sacred energy is dangerous unless we have transmuted our attitudes about sex. It must become genuinely reverenced. We must elevate our attitude toward the opposite sex so that we understand them to be the embodiment of the opposite half of God.

Chapter 26
How Consciousness Creates

In the first Key of the Major Arcana of the Tarot, the adepts gave us a powerful symbolic representation of how consciousness works. This picture, entitled "The Magician," depicts our conscious mind, that portion of our mind that is associated with the objective, rational consciousness. It is the interpreter of our day-to-day experiences. The Magician stands in a posture of focused attention, symbolically drawing the creative power from "above" down into the garden of manifestation. We also see the roses of aspiration and the lilies of realization.

As the picture suggests, the seeds planted from above determine the results, the types of flowers that will blossom. In other words, if we want roses, we must plant roses – not weeds! If we are unhappy with the crop in our garden, it does no good to blame it on someone else. We need to attend to the selection of seeds we are planting and then watering.

The conscious mind, that part of consciousness most people identify with, has the job of selecting those suggestions (i.e. the seeds) that will be planted in the garden of subconsciousness. It is the subconscious mind with its direct connection to the collective unconscious that builds what we call our reality.

The Subconscious Mind

What is the function of our subconscious mind? How does it work? How do we communicate with it? The answer to all these questions involves the importance of symbols.

Paul Case wrote that the subconscious mind evolved at a period before the development of written language. While this is undoubtedly true, the reason that subconsciousness uses symbols and pictures to communicate goes far deeper. To understand this, it is necessary to understand how Western initiates explain the process of manifestation.

The Hermeticists conceived of three major stages of creative activity. This became associated with the Biblical divisions defined as "Body, Mind and Soul." This is usually referred to, in Theology, by the terms: Soma – Body; Psyche – Mind; and, Pneuma – Spirit. This threefold division is the basis for many like classifications in related schools, (Freemasonry, for example, with its Entered Apprentice, Fellowcraft and Master's degrees).

The Qabalists classified this same process according to a four-fold scheme, attributed to the letters of the Tetragrammaton, the four lettered, ineffable name of God – "Yod- Heh-Vav-Heh" (י ה ו ה).

These models illustrate a fundamental difference between exoteric, mainstream physics and the esoteric tradition handed down through the mystical initiatory schools of the Mystery Traditions.

As was pointed out earlier, all causation is postulated to originate within. A pattern is established by a clearly defined image. It is energized by desire force and proceeds to arrange circumstances and events toward manifestation.

Quantum physics has demonstrated that consciousness affects the outcome of experience. Metaphysics has asserted that consciousness influences manifestation. Esoteric teaching and training demonstrates that our reality is created by the selection and energization of images held habitually in our consciousnesses.

As has been emphasized previously, to communicate with the subconscious mind we must use its language, i.e. symbols. Tarot, for example, is an extremely effective tool to train consciousness because it utilizes symbols, many of which are archetypal or universal in nature. These act as matrices for manifestation.

The Qabalistic model may be illustrated by considering the Four Worlds you were introduced to in Chapter Six. These Worlds are attributed to the four letters of the Tetragrammaton of the Hebrews. The following table lists some of the more important attributions associated with this system of classification:

Name of World	English	Direction	Letter	Type of Consciousness	Reality	Element
Atziluth	Divine	South	י Yod,	"I"	Divine	Fire
Briah	Creation	West	ה Heh	"I Am"	Archetypal	Water
Yetzirah	Formation	East	ו Vav	"This is We"	Mythic	Air
Assiah	Manifest	North	ה Heh	"This is Me"	Manifest	Earth

The Hebrew word "olahm" which is translated as "world" is perhaps misleading, since it does not represent a place existing in time or space, but rather a stage or expression of the Divine energy in the creative process. Thus, the four worlds all exist in the same "space" simultaneously.

Perhaps an example, before we go any further, will help clarify our understanding. Let us start with the archetypal concept of "clean." On the level of the second world of Briah or Creation, this would express as those states of consciousness that express these qualities, i.e. Order, Unity and Wholeness. As the focus shifts to express in the third World of Yetzirah or Formation, we see a narrowing of expression represented by several images. For example, we could conceive of the idea of "clean" as expressed by "sweeping," but the manner of this expression could be further narrowed to the use of a "push-broom," a "whisk-broom," a "vacuum cleaner," or even a "dust-cloth." Whichever image is selected becomes manifested in the fourth World of Manifestation, Assiah.

All energy starts as Consciousness in Atziluth. In the world of Assiah we see that all energy manifests through a form. Even in the "shadow borderland" that Quantum Physicists deal with, Light may manifest as particles known as "*photons.*"

PART FOUR

Archetypes

Chapter 27
The Fertile Garden of Consciousness

The traditions preserved in the archives of the esoteric orders tell of a remote period of humanity's prehistory when the infant race was visited by god-like creatures. These entities helped our ancient ancestors make the transition to full Homo sapiens. Some believe these benefactors were ancient astronauts who came to earth in space ships and through genetic engineering stimulated the transformation. This, they say, is where the legends of the great culture gods originated.

Others hold to the theory that these great ones were, and are, our Elder Brothers and Sisters who were products of the evolutionary process of the life-wave immediately preceding ours. These have been called, in some writings that stem from the same source as the Fraternity of the Hidden Light, by the names of

"The Lords of Venus," "The Lords of Sirius," or "The Lords of Mind."

It is related that these "Lords" implanted, by telepathic means, great "seed thoughts" or "Archetypal Patterns" into the group consciousness of the early human race. These symbols, planted in the fertile garden of consciousness, flowered forth to manifest in emerging humanity. These patterns are still unfolding today. Carl Jung described the functioning of these symbols thus:

Archetypes perform very like non-material organs conferring the formal patterns of connection.

These symbols act as a kind of focusing system that carries the patterns of existence from the mind of God. Their function in consciousness is similar to that which DNA performs for the physical body. They carry the "genes" of consciousness, the "coding" of manifestation.

When the initiate becomes a channel for these symbols, he becomes a vehicle of the will, capacities and wisdom originating at this higher level of consciousness. As he progresses upon the path of self-realization, these qualities arise from the inner planes of consciousness as manifestations of the inner wisdom of the Individuality as dynamic images, triggering an awakening into higher experience of self-knowledge. By doing this, the aspirant contacts the powerful group mind of the initiatory path and is enabled to unleash great transformative energies in a safe manner. This experience accelerates his unfoldment and transforms his everyday life experience into the "Great Adventure." Thus, the "pilgrim" experiences a greater zest, sense of joy and energy in his interactions, both inner and outer. His journey is now filled with a renewed sense of purpose that supports him through the challenges that he will face.

The archetypal images are Divine in origin and have their source of power in the realm of Atziluth, which exists beyond the limitations of time, space and the phenomenal world. It is this potency that empowers the figures of "myths." Our ancient brothers and sisters did not invent these symbols for they "were sown in consciousness by the hand of God."

It is through their stories that we can become aware of what has been called "the Great Story" written about by such people as Joseph Campbell, in his work *The Hero with a Thousand Faces.* This story reveals the process of the awakening to the full potency of our souls.

Our consciousness clothes these incredibly potent patterns, themselves composed of conscious energy, in symbolic forms. For example, the energy known as the archangel Michael is usually depicted as a powerful warrior, clad in golden armor with blue eyes, red beard and hair, etc. We should realize that Michael need not and almost certainly doesn't resemble this description. Michael probably is not anthropomorphic in form at all! The point is, that by visualizing and working with this symbolic form, we focus our consciousness and establish at a very deep level the link that is used to evoke this transformative power.

Archetypes are centers of powerful conscious energy that exist deep within the world of the collective consciousness. It has been noted that some of these centers are more active than others in the expression of human consciousness. It seems that they act almost as "time release capsules," timed to become active at different stages of the evolution of both individuals and cultures. Each has a microcosmic correspondence and each is also related to a specific chakra.

Work with these archetypes comprises a major area of concentration and development in the Greater Mysteries. We will go into this in more detail when we discuss them.

Interacting with these symbols is not only important for the individual initiate but also for the culture in which we find ourselves incarnated. We live in a time of great change and great potential. Sages of all periods have pointed to this time as an age of fulfillment! Of all of the souls who could incarnate at this time, we were chosen to help humanity to be born to this new experience. We see everywhere the breakdown of the whole system. We are preparing for the "breakthrough" into a new, expanded, awakened vision of reality. Never more than now is it more important to embrace our potential as co-creators of our universe. Truly, the Work is great, but the hands are few. But remember, there is a blessing upon all who serve!

Chapter 28
If You Don't Go Within – You'll Go Without!

Over the portal of the Temple of the Mysteries at Delphi were emblazoned the words "Know Thy Self!" Such was the purpose of the Mysteries. We would be in error, however, if we supposed that this injunction referred to the acquisition of intellectual knowledge, arrived at through introspection. If such were the case, the Mysteries would have been no more than a school of philosophy, and the initiates could have achieved their goal simply by reading or listening to discourses. There would have been no need for the secrecy or the involved rituals and ceremonial procedures.

If intellectual prowess was not the prize, what was the object of this most venerated of ancient institutions? What, indeed, do the genuine schools of initiation perpetuate to this day?

The word "knowledge" or "know" is one with far-reaching esoteric implications. It is central to the whole mystery tradition. The term "mystery" itself is connected with knowledge. Mystery, in this context, is not identical with its modern usage, as a puzzle to be solved. Rather it comes from a word with the connotation of a type of knowledge that cannot be imparted intellectually, but has to be experienced. Once having received this knowledge, called "Gnosis," the individual is transformed, often quite dramatically. This experience is a spiritual illumination. Examples are found in the life of the Buddha in his awakening under the Bodhi tree and in the Bible with Saint Paul's conversion on the road to Damascus. Here we find experiences that profoundly affected the personalities of the individuals in question, providing a quantum leap in consciousness.

What is the nature of this transformation? Again, this is found in another meanings of the word "Gnosis" or in Hebrew, "Da'ath." In the

Bible we find "knowledge" or "to know" used to mean "union." On the physical level, this is sexual union ("...and Adam knew Eve..." etc.) On the psychic level, it is integration, a harmonious relationship of the different aspects of our consciousness. On the spiritual level, it is Union, or atonement (at-one-ment) – but union with what?

"Know Thy Self," or "Unite," or "become one" with Thy Self. Not the little self of the ego or intellect, but the Self that is our true "I Am." This is the spirit within, the ruler of the "Temple of the Heart!" This Self is synonymous with what we have termed the Individuality. It is this consciousness which is the vehicle for an evolution, as compared to the personality, which is the vehicle that is built up for a single incarnation.

The goal of the Mysteries, therefore, is to so align, balance, and harmonize the consciousness so that the Individuality may descend and take possession of its personality. It is to this transformation that Jesus referred when he stated, "My Father" (the

Individuality), and I (the personality) are one (Gnosis)."

T. S. Elliot, expressed this process in his poem "Little Gidding" (1942) when he wrote:

We shall not cease from our exploring until the end of all of our exploration is to arrive where we started and know the place for the first time.

Chapter 29
The Sense of Symbols

What are symbols? Why are they so lasting, so important? Why do they fascinate us and figure in so many tales of power, mystery and magic?

There is a story about soldiers during the retreat of Napoleon's Great Army following their defeat in Russia. It occurred in the dead of winter. There was nothing but snow, ice and bitter cold. The French soldiers were starving and freezing on the long trek back to France. Any food that had not already been commandeered, any crops that had not already been burned, were scavenged in their attempts to stave off starvation. Every piece of wood that could be found, either in the wild or among the boards from the barns that they came across, was sacrificed to the fire to keep from freezing to death. Every piece of wood, with one notable exception, was burned. The crosses and wood of the numerous roadside shrines were, without exception, spared. The wood that these religious symbols were constructed from would have burned just as well as the other wood, yet it was left unmolested! Why? Because the Soldiers had been conditioned from the time that they had played at their mothers' knees that these symbols were holy and stood for a power greater than their need for temporary warmth! The power of this conditioning, of these symbols, had penetrated deeply into their consciousnesses and had become a foundation upon which their lives, their existence, was built.

To understand the "sense" and power of symbols, we have to understand the dynamics of consciousness. This is important because, be assured, consciousness creates! We must align its creative powers with worthy goals.

Freud, Jung and other depth psychologists brought to the attention of the general public what had long been known and utilized by initiates of the Mystery Traditions, since before the time of Ancient Egypt. The existence and function of certain levels of mind, beyond what is conscious, was postulated and it was considered to extend to the levels of the Collective. This concept revolutionized the science of psychology, but it is not new. The powers of these levels of consciousness were well known to the initiates and adepts of the past.

Eliphas Levi, writing in his *Key to the Mysteries,* during the mid-nineteenth century, described the potency and possibilities of these levels of consciousness as follows:

There exists a force in nature which is far more powerful than steam, by means of which a single man who can master it, and knows how to direct it, might throw the world into confusion and transform its face. It is diffused throughout infinity; it is the substance of heaven and earth. When it produces radiance it is called light. It is substance and motion at one and the same time; it is a fluid and a perpetual vibration. The will of intelligent beings acts directly upon this light, and by means thereof, upon all nature, which is made subject to the modifications of intelligence.

By the direction of this agent we can change the very order of the seasons, produce in the night the phenomena of day, correspond instantaneously from one end of the earth to the other, heal or hurt at a distance, and endow human speech with a universal reverberation and success. To know how to master this agent so as to profit by and direct its currents is to accomplish the Magnum Opus, to be master of the world, and the depository even of the power of God.

Being the instrument of life, this force naturally collects at living centers; it cleaves to the kernel of plants as to the heart of man, but it identifies itself with the individual life of the existence it animates. We are, in fact, saturated with this light, and continually project it to make room for more. The settlement and polarization of this light about a center produces a living being; it attracts all the matter necessary to perfect and preserve it.

This force has four properties – to dissolve, to consolidate, to quicken, and to moderate. The four properties, directed by the will of man, can modify all phases of nature.

(1959. Trans. Aleister Crowley. London: Rider & Co.)

We find these properties amplified again and again in the writings of "New Thought" metaphysicians such as Thomas Troward, Ernest Holmes, and Charles Filmore. Profound as these writings are, they just scratch the surface of the understanding to be experienced in a working lodge of the Western Mysteries.

The Law of Causation

Nothing happens at random, despite what Chaos Theorists may claim. What some term "chaos" or "chance" or "miracles" are simply caused by that which is too complex to be understood. Everything proceeds from a chain of causation.

Where esoteric science differs from its exoteric counterpart is in the recognition of the source of the manifestation process. Materialistic science denies the existence of the unseen realms of consciousness. Esoteric science postulates the principle of "inner causality." All creation, all chains of manifestation are initiated in the worlds of the images. As we have pointed out, this principle places great responsibility upon the individual. No longer can they place the blame for their circumstances on outside potencies, such as the Devil, or God or even other individuals. It also places in the same hands complete control, complete power, within the bounds of karmic ties; power to give us the ability to manifest our destiny and our dreams. The root cause is deep within and it is manifested through our images.

Many have found out to their dismay that the manifestation of our conditions and circumstances does not result from our words and intellectual concepts. Affirmations, no matter how carefully worded will be found to be minimally effective when communicating to our deep consciousness unless they evoke an image.

For example, let us take the instance of someone preparing to give his first speech in front of an audience. It is relatively well known now that according to a survey conducted in the last quarter of the twentieth century, speaking in public is the number one fear of modern American adults. Death was number four! Therefore, we may know that preparing for a speech is accompanied by some trepidation. An individual imagines themselves standing behind a lectern or podium, their knuckles white from the death grip they have on the speaker's stand and they are visibly shaking. This image intrudes repeatedly as they say to themselves –"No! No! No! I'm going to be all right! I'm not going to be afraid! I'm not going to experience stage fright!" They say this vigorously, pouring their emotional fervor into it. They may practice this "affirmation" over and over again.

The day of the actual presentation arrives. They walk to the speaker's stand and look out at the audience. All of a sudden, to their dismay, they find that their mouth has gone dry, breathing becomes shallow and their hands have begun to perspire. They look down and see their knuckles are indeed white from gripping the podium so tightly. "So much for positive thinking!" they muse.

What happened? Did the speaker's subconscious mind malfunction? No, quite the contrary, the subconscious <u>never</u> fails. However, the "speech-giver" didn't speak to it in the proper language. A mixed message was received and acted upon.

As we mentioned earlier, we create our reality through the images we select and choose to energize with our emotions. In our example, the image that was being energized was that of the speaker being paralyzed with stage fright. This image, created in consciousness, was manifested in time and space. The subconscious could not recognize the verbal command, "No!"

Remember, any clear, consistent, energized mental image will tend to manifest itself as an actual condition or event! Thus, our deep consciousness contains the awesome powers of creativity. But how do we control it?

The Law of Response

Subconsciousness is completely and consistently amenable to suggestions, couched in images, originating at the conscious level. We exercise complete dominion over this creative process. That is the challenge that faces us and is the source of most of our problems. When we image half-truths, false limitations, predictions of doom, subconsciousness accepts these "molds of manifestation" as suggestions and blueprints for objectification. We can then say with Job, "What I feared has come upon me."

Subconsciousness responds to those images that are promoted as suggestions rather than commands. As The Emerald Tablet of Hermes puts it, "Suavely and with great ingenuity..." Why is this? Because when we attempt to storm the gates of our deep consciousness by force, our willing and obedient servant reacts as follows: "A lot of effort and force is being used to influence me. I must be difficult to deal with. Therefore, I will be difficult to control!" This could not be farther from the truth. Subconsciousness is completely responsive. We must use discrimination in what instructions we give her. Thus, it is said, "Discrimination is the first virtue on the Path."

Are we then totally responsible for any calamity that befalls us? For example, I knew a lady who was deeply committed to the philosophy of New Thought. Her husband contracted leukemia and passed away. Her "friends" asked her what she had been holding in her consciousness that precipitated this experience. Was she responsible? It all depends on what "she" means. If "she" refers to the Individuality, the greater or higher self, then yes. We are each ultimately responsible for our evolutionary and transformative experiences including karmic repercussions. But if we are referring (and we generally are) to the personality, then we must remember that we not only have the karma of many incarnations, but we also share karma on the familial, genetic, national and race consciousness basis.

In my example, my friend and her husband may well have been going through that experience for the rest of us!

Symbols vs. Signs

Symbol is the language of our deep consciousness. More importantly, it is the common language of the Collective Unconsciousness. A genuine symbol will convey the same meaning to the deep consciousness of one person as it does to any other person, regardless of age, sex, education or intelligence. Difference in comprehension may manifest when the message surfaces to the conscious level. But even there, it will be basically the same. We may meditate on a symbol designed to improve memory and it will improve our memory whether we consciously understand the symbol or not. Thus, contrary to certain mystical schools' teaching on this matter, true symbols have an innate universal meaning.

Signs, on the other hand, depend on an understanding of their meanings and upon agreed convention and function, primarily on the level of the intellect.

Rituals invariably use both signs and symbols, but their effectiveness depends on the correct use and coordination of the latter. Great use is made of "Tables of Correspondences" in the esoteric fraternities. These are basically a cross reference of lists that enumerate various symbol systems. Some belong to sight, some to sound and so forth for all the senses. These are combined and coordinated to form a powerful, dynamic symbol that penetrates to our subconsciousness to produce the desired suggestion. But ceremonial is much more than just a potent autosuggestion, as we shall see later.

The Universe is a continual interplay of one Divine energy moving continuously from various levels of consciousness into different levels of manifestation and back again. As the Emerald Tablet says, "It ascends to Heaven and descends again to Earth …"

Chapter 30
The Magical Library

When our personal images are linked to archetypal potencies, through the medium of our subconsciousness, they will transform us. How is this done? What can we do to facilitate this connection?

Initiates believe that we live in a multi-tiered cosmos. The manifest or physical realm is only the tip of the iceberg. This fact is affirmed, not only by mystics but also by psychologists like C.G. Jung and physicists like Michael Talbot, (see his *Holographic Universe*, 2011). Initiates and adepts have understood how this multi-reality functions in relation to the creative process since ancient times. This process is initiated within. But for creation to exist at all, it must have a return flow. To perpetuate itself, the energy must vibrate between two poles of existence.

As we have discussed, in the Qabalah it is taught that reality is manifested in four "olahms" or worlds:

[1] Atziluth – essence or archetype
[2] Briah – creation
[3] Yetzirah – formation
[4] Assiah – manifestation

Those familiar with the New Testament through the Renaissance will be familiar the three-fold division of "Spirit, Mind and Body." This correlates with the Qabalistic system, however, Atziluth or Deity is the positive pole of our Cosmic Circuit, so it is not considered in the Hermetic or Renaissance system whose focus is on the Microcosm. We have gone into some detail with this discussion in previous chapters because it has direct bearing upon human make-up and the constitution of the inner worlds.

There is one energy, which is God. But this energy functions differently on each of these three levels. We humans relate to each of these realties differently:

LEVEL	TYPE OF REALITY	EXPRESSES AS
Pneuma	Essential or Archetypal	Pure Consciousness
Psyche	Mythic	Symbolic
Soma	Manifest	Form

Manifest Reality

Starting at the level with which we are most familiar, Soma, we find we are dealing with the plane of conditions, effects or appearances. This is the level of manifest reality wherein the creative energy expresses through form. We may direct this energy by choosing to have it flow through chosen forms. This can be further enhanced through the use of color, conductors and crystalline substances. We can see this applied in structures such as the Great Pyramid and the principles of the Chinese science of Feng Shui.

The challenge most people face when dealing with this level is one of identification. They tend to consider this level as "the real world." It is real, contrary to those philosophies that deny this level completely. However, it is not the only reality. In the creative process, it functions as effect, rather than cause. To become attached to any given form invites unhappiness for all manifest forms are transitory and changing from moment to moment. The good news is that these constant transitions may be guided towards improvement, growth and a fuller, more perfect expression of Spirit.

Mythic Reality

"If I say something three times, it is so!"

(Alice in *Through the Looking Glass*).

When Alice fell down the rabbit hole or passed through the looking glass, she made the transition from the world of manifest reality into that of mythic reality. Some would call this the world of fantasy and they would be right – partially. In addition to fantasy, we find myths, literature, folk and fairy tales. Here too are the memories of all civilizations: Sumeria, Egypt, Atlantis and all others since the time of the beginning. The Akashic records also reside at this level.

This is the level of the Collective Unconscious, the Astral Plane, the imagination and memory of nature. It has been called in the Qabalah, the "Treasure House of Images" and the Kingdom of Shades and Hell. We come into contact with this level through our imagination.

Many question the reality of the imagination, equating it with unreality. They dismiss all of the interior realities by saying, "It's only imagination!" But the enormity of their error is revealed when we consider the fact that the creative process is initiated via the vehicle of the imagination.

On the Qabalistic Tree of Life, this faculty is assigned to the sephirah Tiphareth. This sephirah is connected with the ideas about our higher and true Self. This is the Individuality that incarnates various personalities in order to evolve to perfection.

It is through this spiritual gift of the imagination that we build our symbolic, mythic bridge that connects our manifest world of effects with the spiritual world of cause. It is through these images that we contact those powerful, transforming centers of energy known as the archetypes.

Archetypal Reality

We have previously explored the nature of archetypes. It is interesting to note that the ancient tradition states that these patterns were "sown in the consciousness of humanity" by God in the earliest times. Tradition further asserts that these complexes of consciousness, these seeds, were responsible for the mutations that ultimately transformed Homo erectus into Homo sapiens.

Archetypes were known in Ancient Egypt as the "neters," and in Greece as the gods. Both of these ancient civilizations, and others, are commonly thought to be polytheistic. However, the initiated priesthoods knew that there was only one God. They were also completely familiar with these conscious energy complexes that function at the "I Am" level of the cosmic mind. The secret of aligning personal consciousness with these potencies and making contact with them, to effect the transfiguration of the individual in order to reach full potential, has never been lost to the initiates of the Mystery Schools.

Some of these powers seem to be set to awaken into potency at certain predetermined stages in humanity's evolution of consciousness. The "cosmic genes" then facilitate a quantum leap in conscious evolution to a new expression or stage. This is referred to in the tradition as the movement from one "root race" to another. Arcane tradition asserts that just such a transformation is about to occur. A movement to a new expression of human consciousness.

The Inner Library

Symbols, especially those that are images of the archetypes, are the language of consciousness. They facilitate the energy flow between the worlds. In addition, symbols have a life of their own. They act like seeds planted in the fertile soil of our subconsciousness. There they cause transformations as they are elaborated into networks of ideas, realizations and insights.

Because of this, most legitimate mystery schools direct their students to steep themselves in those writings that make use of this symbology, as may be found in mythology, fantasy or science fiction. Also, students are encouraged to familiarize themselves with traditional symbol systems such as those found in the Tarot, Tree of Life, astrology, alchemy, etc. In this way the common alphabet of the mysteries, the "language of the angels" helps train and forges the consciousness of the adept.

The Magical Alphabet

Many consider "myths" to be synonymous with fantasy or fiction. But for initiates, myths are stories wherein symbols represent cosmic powers. The late Joseph Campbell, the great authority on mythology, points out that mythic themes are universal. Myths use archetypal symbols to bridge the energies of the actual archetypes from the Briatic world, across Yetzirah, to make them accessible to our consciousness. Eventually these "power-paths" manifest in Assiah, the world of time and space.

To facilitate this "bridging" initiates must "stock the library of their consciousness." The various symbols and alphabets that they memorize are intended to serve as meditation subjects so that they may build the paths and establish a language that deep consciousness may use to communicate with its ordinary self-conscious counterpart and vice versa. The ultimate purpose is to establish avenues in the consciousness of the individual initiate, or sometimes in group consciousness, for the expression of the archetypal powers.

Aleister Crowley complained that after being sworn to oaths of secrecy with dire penalties should he break them, he was entrusted with the Hebrew alphabet! If his ego had not gotten in the way at the time and had he reflected upon what he was being given, his comments would have most certainly been different. However, he was, after all, young and inexperienced.

The Hebrew alphabet, for example, is much more than a series of letters. When one studies the characteristics of this foundational system of the Western Mysteries as they come down to us from the Near Eastern traditions, certain prominent features become evident. First, this system of symbols did not originate with the nomadic tribes, but was adopted or imparted from elsewhere, perhaps Babylon. It is referred to as the "Chaldee Flame Alphabet." Secondly, it is both phonetic and hieroglyphic.

For example, the first letter, "Aleph," is pronounced phonetically as "ah," or more correctly, a relaxed exhalation. But it is also the sign or symbol for "the ox" and all the ideas that are related to this animal. How does it represent an ox? After only a short period of meditation on this idea, we see how the letter, as usually depicted today, is really a stylized picture of this animal. The little mark on the top of the letter even represents the small bird, which often accompanies the beast, picking bugs from its back!

The letter "Heh" which is pronounced like an "H" in English also means "window."

ה

Remember that in this part of the world, windows were first associated with tent-flaps and you may see the connection.

Some other examples are:

ל   י   כ

Lamed = ox-goad;   Yod = hand;   Kaph=fist.

These are just a few examples.

The alphabet is arranged and divided according to universal proportions. Take, for example, the division of the letters into their three main groups:

The Mothers

א Aleph – The Element of Air

מ Mem – The Element of Water

ש Shin – The Element of Fire.

These may be assigned to the first three Qabalistic Worlds that we have discussed previously. Aleph = Yetzirah, Mem = Briah, and Shin = Atziluth. As we shall see later, this cross-references with the letters of the "Holy Ineffable Name," the Tetragrammaton.

The Doubles

ב	Beth	B or V	Mercury	Crown Chakra
ג	Gimel	G or J	Moon	Pituitary
ד	Daleth	D or Dh	Venus	Throat
כ	Kaph	K or Ch	Jupiter	Solar Plexus
פ	Peh	P or F	Mars	Genitals
ר	Resh	Er or R	Sun	Heart
ת	Tav	Th or T	Saturn	Sacrum

One of the more profound points of this series is that, when proceeding from the bottom of the list to the top (i.e. starting with Tav and ending with Beth), it provides what is considered by many genuine mystery schools to be the correct esoteric sequence for the awakening of the chakras. You will note that this disagrees with the order given in any number of "New Age" books.

The Simples

The remaining letters are called "Simples." There are twelve of these and they align with the twelve signs of the zodiac and its accompanying and vast system of symbolic correspondences.

They are assigned as follows:

ה	Heh	Aries
ו	Vav	Taurus
ז	Zain	Gemini
ח	Cheth	Cancer
ט	Teth	Leo
י	Yod	Virgo
ל	Lamed	Libra

231

נ	Nun	Scorpio
ס	Samekh	Sagittarius
ע	Ayin	Capricorn
צ	Tzaddi	Aquarius
ק	Qoph	Pisces

The sequence of the 22 letters, with their attributions, allows for what is known in the Fraternity as the "Incarnatory Tableau." By taking the letter assigned to a "sun sign" and the letter assigned to an "ascendant," and following a mathematical formula, we arrive at a set of letters. Their corresponding Tarot trumps reveal much about the purpose of a given incarnation. For those interested in further information about this tableau, I would refer them to "The Threshold," one of the correspondence courses offered to Probationers of The Fraternity of the Hidden Light (See Appendix).

The Tetragrammaton

The letters of the Divine Name, יהוה, are connected with what is probably the most significant set of attributions in the Qabalistic system. Not only do these four letters correlate with the four worlds, but also with the four ancient elements and the four suits of the minor arcana of the Tarot.

This elemental division links a whole host of correspondences such as the seasons, the directions, etc., that may be used with the diagram known as the "Circled Cross," used as the basis of many ritual systems. This symbol, with its four quarters and a single point at the center is surrounded by its limitless circumference. It is one of the oldest symbols and one of the most balanced. The late adept, W. G. Gray, developed much advanced training in connection with this fourfold division (See *Magical Ritual Methods. 1988. Helios, Cheltenham, England*).

Briefly, the Circled Cross symbolically recognizes the truth that we are, in fact, the center of our universe. That is, our true self-creation proceeds outward. Remember, reality has been defined, poetically by the Qabalists, as the great circle whose center is everywhere and circumference is nowhere. This is an image that will repay meditation.

In the following table, we have provided the reader with a selection of attributions for this four-fold system:

Some Qabalistic Correspondences

The Archangels of the Quarters

East	Raphael	"Healing of God"
West	Gabriel	"Strength of God"
South	Michael	"Like unto God"
North	Auriel	"Light of God"

Symbols have a life of their own

Why is it so important that we "sow the field" of our personal consciousness with the seeds of symbols and myths? At the turn of the 19th century and for the first couple of its decades, "dream books" were very popular. With these books, their authors claimed, a person could interpret their dreams.

For example, one would dream of cats and the next morning consult the book to find that cats were associated with our wild, repressed urges longing to be set free. Not only were the meaning of these symbols arbitrarily determined, but the authors totally ignored the uniqueness of each individual. Considering these significant shortcomings, we might guess that these manuals were of little or no use. However, surprisingly enough, it was found that once an individual had used their particular manual for a period of time, satisfying results occurred. It seemed that with practice at using any given system, the personal subconscious of the practitioner adjusted to the symbolic alphabet of the book.

This points out a fact long known by initiates. Not only do symbols communicate with our deep consciousness, they alter it. This is sometimes referred to as "building power paths." Symbols act like "seeds" falling onto the fertile, receptive earth of our subconsciousness. There they germinate and flower forth, often in amazing ways.

This mechanism explains the phenomenon of "initiation" to a large extent as it occurs in authentic mystery vehicles. The symbols, implanted powerfully during the ceremonial and meditative exercises undertaken by each Neophyte, build paths connecting the mundane consciousness with the potent energy complexes of the archetypes. Like connecting a circuit to a power source, the lights of illumination and the engines of mystical powers are put into motion. This "hooking up" process is usually completed only when the next stage is initiated. It is often said that only the taking of the next activates the powers of the previous grade. This phenomenon has been repeatedly validated in the Fraternity of the Hidden Light.

This brings us to one final consideration. It concerns what is referred to in Christian Esoteric Mysticism as the "Mystery of the Crucifixion." Much talk is bandied about with regard to the Master Jesus taking on the accumulated karma of humanity during his sacrificial experience. Many aspirants find this difficult to resolve with their feelings of personal responsibility or karmic debt. May I suggest that what, in fact, the Master accomplished upon the cross was the initial building of the power paths that now link the "Christ Archetype" with the collective consciousness of all humanity, thereby making the energy of this redeeming consciousness available to all.

Chapter 31
The Initiation of Water

A wise engineer once observed, "Anything works on paper!" He was pointing out that, no matter how brilliant a theory is, it must be proven in the "laboratory of life" before it can be considered valid. Thus, the Latin title of the grade of water is "Practicus" meaning "one who practices." This is further emphasized by the Hebrew title of "Baal Omen" or "Master of Truth" or "Faithful Master." The object of the practices of the grade is to prove what has been known previously in theory only.

The Water initiation is often referred to as the "Hermetic" or "Qabalistic" initiation. Its watery symbolism is intended to instruct us on the properties and laws of mind. The mind stuff is said to flow, like a river; to take forms, like water in a glass or bowl. It moves in vortexes, pools, currents, etc.

All forms of manifestation, whether mental or physical, are veils for the One Thing. Modern physicists in the doctrine of "String Theory" have dramatically affirmed this. In the Chaldean Oracles, a Neo-Platonic document believed to have been written about the first century of the Common Era, we read, "Seek ye the river of the soul, whence and in what order ye have come." Note the water symbolism. Manifestation as the great goal and product of the creative process leads naturally back to the starting point, the source.

We shall see that all forms of manifestation reveal the One Power expressing itself through a limited series of geometrical forms. For example, salt and lead are both associated symbolically with crystals that invariably express as cubical structures. These geometrical structures are known among the forms called the "Platonic Solids." In the grade of water, initiates devote much time to studying how these solids and the two mathematical values of "pi" and "phi", known as the irrationals, interact and manifest throughout nature.

Through the conscious mind's ability to direct the currents of the mental "watery" substance by the power of concentrated imagery, the initiate gradually obtains the skill to direct manifestation.

Yet the aspirant must strive for a higher level than this. He must seek to become aware of the fact that he is a vehicle for his Higher Self, the Individuality. He must integrate the realization, "Not my will, but Thine be done," into his habitual thinking patterns. With this practice the individual initiate will become the "Mediating Intelligence," he will consciously strive to become a channel for the higher powers. In Magic, this is known as "Theurgy" which means "god working."

Understanding the basic principles of Theurgy is one of the disciplines that occupies an initiate of this grade. This will be elaborated in succeeding chapters.

Chapter 32
The Symbol in Action

Let us not make the easy mistake of thinking symbols and images are only visual. Symbols can be found that appeal to each of the senses. This is, in fact, the basis for ceremonial. Paul Foster Case, writing in one of his many excellent works on esotericism, stated emphatically that of all the methods available to modern man for spiritual development, ritual and ceremonial was undoubtedly the most powerful.

While I feel that meditation must be the foundational discipline of any spiritual regimen, unless you can retire to an ashram for five to seven years where you concentrate on it full time, your progress may be very slow.

This is one reason we combine the three elements of study, meditation and ceremonial in our probationary program in the Fraternity of the Hidden Light. We find this creates a synergy that not only accelerates development in a safe way, but also helps balance the individual psyche of the aspirant.

Ritual generates energies in a powerful, dynamic way not found in other methods. Dion Fortune liked to compare this approach to the functions of radio reception. She compared the energies from the Inner Plane Hierarchies to a radio signal being transmitted from a distant transmitter. The individual aspirant is the receiver. The signal is being heard, in most cases as being weak, distorted and with static. There are two ways to overcome this problem. She points out: (1) you can increase the power of the signal by getting a stronger transmitter, or (2) you can increase the sensitivity of the receiver by various means such as getting a better antenna. The first she correlates with the use of ritual; the second can be accomplished by fasting, a vegetarian diet and long periods of meditation in retreat. She then identifies the remedies applied by the Western Tradition and the Eastern Tradition respectively.

Much change has taken place in both the energies being broadcast from the Inner Planes and the subtle make-up of the psyches of aspirants since the 1920s when Dion Fortune did her work. We are, in fact, the recipients of "global" traditions now. Still, ritual does remain the most powerful of attunement and transformative technique.

How does ritual accomplish this? We have discussed how symbol, especially when emotionally charged, affects our deep consciousness. Realizing this, consider for a moment the power of a multi-sensory symbol; a symbol that not only appeals to the sense of sight, but also communicates to the subconscious mind via sound, scent, taste and touch. This would be a symbol that is three dimensional and dynamic, a symbol the aspirant experiences in the world of time and space. A ceremony is just that – and more. In ritual we have several symbols that are all attuned to the same keynote. It stimulates the deep consciousness of the individual or group to build a chain of imagery in the Yetziratic World that allows the energy to bridge the gap from the plane of consciousness to the plane of manifestation.

The Egregore

We have all seen the western movie scene where the lynch mob gathers around the outside of the frontier jail with the intent of taking the sometimes innocent, but always unpopular, prisoner for the purposes of "stringing him up." The sheriff faces them down with the famous line, "I can't get you all, but I'll get the first. Who wants to volunteer?"

As stereotypical as that illustration is, the sad truth is that it is probably based upon many factual incidents. What happens when normal, law-abiding folks become a lynch mob? They have become part of a group mind, ensouled by an artificial elemental, a thought construct fueled by strong emotion, originating at a primitive level. When the sheriff called them back to individual responsibility and the possible consequences of their actions, the group "mob" mind disintegrated.

With the mob, the group mind is built up quickly but has no staying power. The group mind of an esoteric order, usually referred to, as the "egregore" is considerably more permanent, especially when reinforced with ritual. It is not uncommon for initiates to reincarnate and pick up the contacts of their old system. They come back on the path and find the same system, even if it has fallen into abeyance, and pick up the vestiges of the supposedly extinct expression. They then experience rapid growth and vitality because they have succeeded in picking up the contacts of an egregore that continues to function. This group-mind is connected with the consciousness of previous adepts and initiates. If it is on the right hand path of light, it can be a great aid for its members.

Chapter 33
The Power of Patterns

All life is a pattern. Our personal patterns determine how well we relate to the rest of existence. When life seems to be in a state of conflict with our environment and its inhabitants, we are advised to examine the patterns and the images that our outer world is based upon. If we bring our inner kingdom into harmony, the outer world will rearrange itself to reflect this inner state.

Some may object to this formula, stating that it confuses the subjective with the objective. But does it? Or, is this a symptom of the delusion of separation? The outer world is our checkpoint. How are we manifesting? We are in control. We are responsible. To the extent that we have identified our personal will with the One Will, we will find it to be free!

When some aspect of our life is out of balance, how do we bring it back into alignment with the Source? In the esoteric traditions, great use is made of symbolic patterns; the Tree of Life, of course, is our primary example of such a pattern. There are others, however, that the spiritual aspirant should explore. Another of these patterns is known as the "mandala." These are used as focuses for meditation, pathworkings or similar deep meditation work and ritual. One of the most basic among this type is the circle cross that you were introduced to earlier.

In all probability, this symbol is related to the most ancient of temples. The local shaman or holy person would choose a suitable place and stick their magical staff into the ground. A length of cord, perhaps the wise one's belt, would be fastened by one end to the staff and the other end to a knife or "athame." A circle would then be drawn using the cord as the radius and marking out the circumference of the sacred place by cutting it into the ground. The path of the sun, from the point of dawn to its setting, defined one diameter. Another diameter would be drawn perpendicular to the first.

Within this symbol, the patterns that are used in ninety percent of the rituals of the Western Tradition can be found. The circle is a symbol of eternity, having neither beginning nor end. It is also an emblem of the one, unchanging, constant reality. Therefore, in the circle, the Ancient Ones found a fitting hieroglyph for Spirit. The equal armed cross has always symbolized the four elements and the material universe. Thus, together the cross and circle symbolize the union of the physical with the spiritual. The points where the arms of the cross touch the circle may each be assigned to one of the four ancient elements while the point at the center of the cross is attributed to the One Identity. It is also symbolic of the "spindle of the wheel," that point in consciousness where contact is made between the worlds and the Divine energy is mediated.

As we mentioned before, this symbol is used as a pattern that is the basis of ceremony. By working according to a balanced pattern we can equilibrate our own imbalances.

In order to work effectively with this mandala, we must assign, or perhaps "discover" would be a more descriptive term, a number of attributions to various parts of the diagram. Assigning these symbols is not enough, however. This is especially true if we are simply using attributions suggested by others or by books. We must work meditatively with each set of attributions, work with them until they become linked in our consciousness and hold meaning for us.

The reader is referred to the table on page 237 where we gave a suggested series of "starter attributions." Notice that we said "starter attributions." These are just on the elementary level. A serious student will go on to develop further connections or relationships and then apply this system of attributions in the selection of balancing meditations, pathworkings, or ritual patterns.

To illustrate how this might work, let us take the case of a fictional probationer. This particular student, upon self-analysis, finds that he or she has early success in their studies, but soon seems to get mired in routine. The typical response to this is to give up and switch to another area of study where this pattern is repeated. The list reveals membership in many organizations, groups and societies. The probationer has seldom lasted beyond the introductory phases. They explains this by stating that they are still at the stage of "The Seeker" and have just not found their "spiritual home." They have been disappointed repeatedly in the leaders and teachings of the various organizations they have come in contact with.

By referring to the diagram of the circled cross, they would perhaps find a possibility of a deficiency in the qualities expressed in the earth quarter. Here we find the attributions of "Rebirth and Persistence." Indeed, "Persistence" and "Stability" are the watchwords of the northern segment of the circle. Working with the "Earth" energies might change this aspirant's point of view. It might aid in developing these qualities and skills that would help them over the initial dry spot and bring them to the realization that, perhaps the problem is not with the teachings with which they have come into contact, but with a lack of consistent practice.

The student can work out individual applications for themselves.

Chapter 34
Ritual Magic and Ceremonial

The adept Dion Fortune defined magic as "the art of causing changes in consciousness at will." Another adept, Paul Case, defined the subject as "the art of determining the forms and shapes which shall be taken in the outer world by the veil of Reality..." And the Fraternity of the Hidden Light defines Magic as "The art of producing desired effects, initiated by changes in consciousness, by directing or aligning with the secret forces of the Cosmos."

One of the first things that is readily apparent from even a casual reading of these definitions is that what the average person thinks of when he hears the word "magic" bears very little resemblance to what the initiate of the Western Mystery Tradition understands by this term. The effects of the stage illusionist or the black mass found in occult thrillers bears little relation to the science of inner creation understood by the adepts.

The word "magic" is commonly thought to come from the ancient Persian language and has its origin in the term "Magi" the priestly caste of the Zoroastrian religion. The three Wise Men in the Epiphany legend in the Bible were traditionally Magi. In the ten grades of initiation in the Western Mysteries assigned to the Tree of Life, you will remember, the next to the highest is called 9=2, "Magus." The activity assigned to this level is Wisdom. Thus, we may infer that Magic is "the Science of the Wise." As studied and practiced in the Fraternity of the Hidden Light, it is quite similar in many respects to a very advanced form of practical psychology.

The Emerald Tablet of Hermes states that the Great Work, the regeneration of consciousness, is performed ". . . suavely and with great ingenuity . . ." Subconsciousness tends to resist demands but will respond readily to hints and suggestions, especially when those suggestions are presented in visual form through symbols. As my good friend and colleague "Daniel" explains in his book, *Way of the Celestian,* (School of Light, 1986, page 2) ". . . Symbols are the language of subconsciousness . . . Basically one could say that a symbol . . . as used in the abstract, is a representation of some profound truth, doctrine or cosmic event; an emblem; a type; as the sword is a symbol of conflict, war; the oak a symbol of strength; white a symbol of purity."

He further states: ". . . one must remember not to focus the attention solely on the symbol itself; the symbol is the associative link which calls the attention to the truth which it represents."

Such suggestions become especially potent when the symbols presented depict concepts from the archetypal levels. For example, a suggestion to enhance the acquisition of Wisdom will be more effective if the symbol of the "Wise Old Man," is used.

A properly constructed magic ceremonial will present a multi-sensory symbol that will provide a potent image to the inner mind. Ceremonial initiation, a form of magic, attunes and adjusts the physical vehicle and its subtle counterparts, including the subconscious, to desired rates of vibratory force. These corresponding parts of the aspirant's vehicle may be awakened and developed through a process similar to resonance, as with a tuning fork and a piano string.

A thorough knowledge of the correspondence of symbols to archetypal energies is fundamental and is necessary in order to construct effective "ritualistic suggestions." These symbolic correspondences and their tables of cross-reference are among the more closely guarded secrets of the initiates of the esoteric fraternities. Some have been published but contain "blinds" or incorrect attributions, possibly to confuse or sabotage the untrained.

While it is certainly true that in the more elaborate forms of ceremonial, certain implements, furnishings, etc. are used, none of these outer reminders are indispensable. The experienced practitioner does not depend upon these aides for successful results. While the true magician will develop a love for and will certainly attempt to surround himself with beautiful things, these are not required for the practice of his art.

The "things" do not have any inherent magical power in and of themselves. I knew an adept who worked most of her rituals in her imagination while lying down on her bed and she was consistently successful! Remember all of the symbols of ritual are designed to reinforce a sharp mental image or suggestion of the effect we desire. These images become thought forms that act as patterns through which the power of the Inner takes form in the outer.

An effective ritual presents a potent suggestion to our consciousness. It builds a thought form through the utilization of all the senses. Vision is stimulated by symbols; taste by wine, salt and bread, etc.; hearing by the chants; smell by the perfumes and incenses; touch by the robes worn and implements held. Mental images become much more potent because they are evoked in a multitude of ways.

A ritual's efficiency depends to a large extent upon the operator's understanding of what he says and does. Going through the motions of a ritual without understanding why we are carrying out each step soon reduces its high science to the level of superstition. A caution is appropriate here for the would-be magician. Many novices or groups of novices decide to "do ritual" without a firm grounding in valid theory. They attempt to become experts by reading a few good books on the subjects. Just as ritual can provide a strong suggestion for good, an incorrectly constructed or poorly executed ceremonial can be harmful. While in most cases, a ritual performed incorrectly will not be effective, it may, in some instances, cause distinct problems through poor suggestions. For example, color and sound are particularly potent for healing, but also for harming. As my friend Robert Wang, author of *The Qabalistic Tarot* remarked to me, "Many people think color and sound are merely symbolic, but they aren't symbols – they are actual forces!"

Another warning is appropriate. The force invoked in magic is neutral. It may be used for good or for antisocial purposes. Initiates realize that misuse of these potencies carries a horrible price. It cannot be stressed enough that the excuse that "the ends justify the means" is a trap that leads to the left hand path. When we remember that the personal vehicle of the magician is the channel and amplifier of these forces, we understand how this path, also called black magic, leads surely and inescapably to the physical and psychological deterioration of the magician.

Some people object to the use of a fixed pattern and find it distasteful in relation to their efforts toward spiritual unfoldment. They might say that they prefer a free-flowing process of realization. But, the fact is, few people can hold a thought form clearly enough and long enough to change old habits without the help of a structured pattern.

Another objection that is sometimes voiced is that ritualistic magic unnecessarily complicated. Some will say, "Why not just meditate and 'affirm' our intention?" While we would not discount the importance of either the practice of meditation or an affirmation, we realize that few people are such expert visualizers or can express themselves so powerfully in verbal form as to be able to make the necessary impression upon the inner consciousness. When we make a symbolic gesture we tell our subconsciousness what would take pages to put into words. Paul Case once made the following observation, that when a magician performs a ritual, "…he makes a mental pattern which is like a painting in full color, whereas visualization or spoken words are like a pencil sketch."

Chapter 35
Constructing the Form

Let us "build" a magical ritual to serve as an example and apply our theory as discussed thus far. The first point to examine is known as "the intention" of the rite. It is the purpose of the ceremony. Most failures occur because the goal of the endeavor is not clearly formulated. When we don't know where we are going, we shouldn't be surprised if we don't get there! The intention is the key, because it guides all decisions that follow. The entire ritual is built around this central core.

In this example, we choose as our intention, the improvement of our powers of concentration. By referencing what we know about the Tree of Life we realize that the power of concentration is connected to the complex of ideas related to the sephirah Hod, or Splendor on the Tree. Then, referencing a set of Tables of Correspondence, such those found in Dion Fortune's *Mystical Qabalah,* or Gareth Knight's *Practical Outline of Qabalistic Symbolism,* or perhaps Crowley's *777,* we may proceed to compose a ritual using those correspondences listed for Hod.

Our temple and altar will therefore be draped in orange. The number eight should be featured, perhaps in the number of knocks used, circumambulations, or the number of candles. Our incense would probably be sandalwood, the incense associated with Mercury. We would wear orange or yellow robes and upon our breasts we would display an eight-sided design bearing the Caduceus of Hermes, (best known as the symbol of the medical profession) because it is the staff that Hermes or Mercury carries. Referencing the Tarot, we could use images associated with Tarot Key #1, The Magician, the card that is assigned to Mercury. This should give the average student an idea of how to use the correspondence tables. For your information, I have included the main correspondences for Hod below.

Correspondences of Hod

Hod, Splendor. Located at the base of the Pillar of Severity at the left angle of the Triangle of Personality. Known as the "Perfect Intelligence," the intellect or lower mind. Its magical image is a Mercury type figure or a Hermaphrodite.

GOD-NAME: Elohim Tzabaoth
ARCHANGEL: Raphael
PALACE: Mercury
SYMBOLS: The Caduceus, Octagon, Octagram, Octahedron, the Water Cup, and the Apron.
METAL: Mercury.
MICROCOSMIC: Lower legs.
INCENSE: Mastic, mace and storax (sandalwood).
PRIMARY COLOR: Orange (Yellow for Key #1)

Although many initiates have dedicated rooms in their houses or apartments for ritual work, in this day and age of smaller living quarters, it is not necessary. Any room temporarily cleared of furniture can be used as a temple, with a clean bed sheet to act as a floor cloth. Any small table will serve as an Altar. A Cordelier or apron of the proper color can substitute as a robe. In this way the serious student can take advantage of these instructions right away without having to wait until he has gathered together all of the implements and without a great expenditure of money. The initiate can use these few physical props as reminders to visualize him or herself as being in a grand temple with exquisite implements and flowing robes.

It is better to have one good, pleasing cordelier than a dozen robes you feel are inadequate. High quality instruments are not acquired overnight. In fact, the initiate themselves, during the course of their training, constructs most of the major implements. A polished product is not as important as one that results from their best efforts. Only the best is good enough for service to the Higher Powers.

The initiate begins by conveying the intent of the ceremony to deep consciousness. They start by meditating upon the goal and by reading inspirational writings dedicated to the theme. They would perhaps look at the Tarot Key corresponding to their intention. In our present example he would meditate upon Key #1, "The Magician" assigned to the function of attention and concentration.

A purifying bath, using water that contains a little salt, is traditional. The intent should be to cleanse the mind and emotions as well as the body in preparation for the ritual. The initiate then dons clean clothes, the cordelier or robe, while holding the chosen purpose clearly in mind at all times during this process. Every act should be done with of the intention of the ritual in mind.

The aspirant now enters their temple, or whatever prepared place they are using. Upon entering, the stated intention is said aloud. The following formula is an example: "I will apply all of my powers to align myself with the Divine forces of the Cosmos, to achieve the following aim: to improve my powers of concentration so that I may become a better channel for the Primal-Will-to-Good; and I hereby perform this ceremony to that end."

Other words may be used but it is important to state the intention clearly and in an audible voice.

The next step is known as "preparation of the place." This is a symbolic cleansing and sealing of the temple. By doing this, the practitioner is mirroring an inner process. This is a cardinal principle in ritual: <u>All outer actions represent inner processes.</u> In this case, the process concentrates and purifies inner consciousness, in preparation for the work ahead.

Next, this is accomplished by the performance of one of the various "Banishing Rituals." These differ from one organization to another. The initiate would then pace the circle. This is done by walking around the perimeter of the working space, first with Water and then with Fire. With Water, the aspirant would sprinkle water from a cup towards the East, then South, West and finally North, with the intention of cleansing the "atmosphere" of the place. With Fire, they would walk with either a censor or a stick of incense in the same manner for the purpose of consecrating, i.e. "making sacred" the area. It is important in all three of these activities to "complete the circle of the place." What we mean by this is simply to finish where you started, in the East, so that a full circle will be walked in each of these operations.

When this preparation is accomplished, the initiate proceeds to the "invocation." This invocation is basically a prayer of petition, calling down the particular aspect of power that corresponds to the intention. In our example, we would feature the Divine Name of Hod which is, "Elohim Tzabaoth." This translates as "Creative Power of Hosts."

The technical knowledge necessary for the proper intonation of these Names has never been published outside the orders and we may not discuss them in this book, save to say that they are part of the training given to initiates of the inner levels of the Fraternity of the Hidden Light. For the purpose of this work we would recommend chanting the names on one note, whichever note is most comfortable for the aspirant.

The effect of the invocation should be to so exalt the consciousness of the magician and "enflame with prayer", as the semi-legendary adept Abra-Melin says, that his concentration becomes one-pointed and makes a doorway between the Inner and the Outer worlds.

At this point, we would visualize the "Magical Image" of Hod, which is a Mercury type figure, standing before us. This visualization acts as what is technically known in the Mysteries as a "Telesmatic Image" that functions in the manner of an energy converter. We stop here to wait a few minutes. If we have done our job well, a potent suggestion will be made. Even if no apparent effect is consciously experienced at the moment, the ritual will have done its work and will manifest later in our daily lives.

The aspirant should not be content to perform this ceremony only one time. If repeated on a regular basis, more dramatic results will occur. The initiate may arrive at the climax of the ceremony many times with no obvious results. However, one day, poised between the worlds, he will experience the descent and influx of the power. Then he will look upon "achieving powers of concentration" from an entirely new point of view. He will know! He will speak as one who is in authority for he will have, for possibly only a split second in eternity, become the Divine, channeling the power of concentration through the vehicle that is his personality.

The next part of the ceremony is an act of thanksgiving, a prayer of praise and gratitude. Then we release the "wards" that we set during the preparation of the place with the intention of freeing the currents to return to their normal functions. To expand the consciousness in the temple is one thing. To attempt to drive down a busy street in this condition is quite another manner. Forgetting the release will, at the very least, cause you to have trouble falling asleep.

For the energies to do their greatest good they must be "earthed." This means worked into the densest of our vehicles – the physical body. The practices of going through a series of physical exercises to tense and relax the muscles and then eating following the ceremony are important. Both serve to integrate the effects of the ceremony into our physical vehicles.

It is important to sit down as soon as is practical and write a record of our experiment. Just as exoteric scientists keep careful journals of their work, so should the esoteric scientist follow this practice. By doing this immediately following the ritual, we may catch many insights that, like dreams, will rapidly fade with the passage of time.

In the end, our awareness of the magical nature of all of life becomes enhanced. We see and understand the "dance of creation, preservation, transformation and resurrection" that goes on around and through us. Then, we will continually experience the miracle of being, the magic of the moment.

Chapter 36
Meditation:
The Foundation of the Temple

"Without the regular practice of meditation, performed in an efficient manner, any real achievement in spiritual realization is impossible."

(*The Threshold*, lesson #17, p.1)

Meditation is an indispensable part of the discipline of the Mysteries to awaken the mind to higher consciousness. In some popular explanations of meditation, the student is taught to relax and daydream, often with the aid of a mantra. The fact that so many people have found such a simple technique to be highly beneficial is a reflection of the magnitude of the tension and stress that many people experience in their lives. Indeed, relaxation is a prerequisite for effective meditation, but there is much more to be gained from true meditation than the release of physical and emotional strain.

In the Mysteries, initiates are taught to use meditation to attune the mind to states of conscious knowledge above the personality level. True meditation involves holding a specific image. This chosen image is called the focus. To be able to hold the focus, we must evoke a desire to know more about it. The Tarot or Rota, as it is known in the esoteric fraternities, builds this skill in a positive manner. Unfortunately, most people outside the Mysteries equate the Tarot with fortune telling and the uninitiated use of these sacred symbols has made them the target of ridicule. But properly used, Tarot is one of the most effective tools for developing the capacity to participate in the consciousness of higher levels of awareness.

Our consciousness may be thought of as a cup. It must be receptive to that which is above. In true meditation we ask a definite question. This galvanizes our desire and activates our subconscious forces around the particular phase of knowledge connected with our meditational focus. Subconsciousness will then supply related ideas for conscious assessment. When this focus is concerned with an aspirational yearning, a questing, it becomes a call to the Higher Self for the unveiling of some particular principle of Truth. After this call is sounded in the inner worlds, we continue to hold this focus in quiet expectation of the answer.

During this process, we must hold the mind constantly on our chosen subject and the related questions without wavering. By limiting the field of observation, the whole force of attention is brought to bear on the image that has been chosen as the focal point of the meditation. An ancient metaphor likens the mind to a pool. When the water is turbulent, only surface appearances can be observed. But when the water is still, it becomes clear and one may see into the depths. By controlling our thoughts, the pool of the mind is stilled, allowing realizations to be garnered, through the vehicle of subconsciousness, that have their source in higher levels.

We may reason that an essential skill, which must be present before meditation can be successfully pursued, is the power to concentrate. When asked about gaining skill in concentration, one of my teachers always responded, "Do you know how to worry? If you can worry, and who has failed to be a genius at worrying, then certainly you know how to concentrate." To concentrate, we simply focus on one thought or idea. When we are worried, we may try to remove our attention from the problem, but usually with little success! Therefore, there is nothing wrong with our ability to keep consciousness focused on one thing, is there? The problem is that the untrained use of our powers has often been directed toward producing those results that we do not want. We can transmute this power to concentrate, formerly expressed as the act of worrying, into a more controlled, positive manifestation.

When we are anticipating an important event, whether it is something happy or not happy, we concentrate without effort. We find, however, that when we attempt to concentrate on something that is not really important to us, our attention will tend to wander. We may struggle with ourselves, but we will have little success in getting our power of attention to remain concentrated on any focal point that holds no interest for us. The consciousness will automatically float to the area of our true interest. It will do no good to lie to ourselves. Subconsciousness is not fooled by words that contradict our feelings and actions.

As we have stressed earlier, subconsciousness is best directed by using pictorial images, so our focus should be presented in that form. There isn't anything we think or feel that doesn't have a certain kind of pictorial image involved. These images carry an emotional charge. Mental concentration cannot be divorced from feeling. The desire levels provide the motivating power of the mind, and as we develop our emotional levels we will find we have more power at our disposal. People who exalt the intellect above all else and disparage the feeling and emotional side of themselves cut themselves off from the roots of life.

Concentration and meditation are not intellectual processes alone. You cannot pay attention to anything unless you are interested. Concentration will only remained focused upon that which we care about. When we *feel* a true need to know more about something, our consciousness will focus successfully. Some people think of emotion as an unevolved expression of consciousness that must be overcome. This error causes many problems. It is true that when one's life is completely controlled by the emotions, instability results. But the consequences are just as unpleasant if any other vehicle of the personality is allowed to have unbalanced control. It is the Higher Self that is the true driver of our vehicles. The personality is composed of physical and etheric bodies, subconsciousness, intellect and emotions. These must be balanced and consciously placed under the perfect control of our True Self.

The meditative process focuses the attention in a specifically designated area and then uses the image-making faculty to actively create and provide a channel for certain answers. Thus, meditation is a creative process.

We really do not have to learn how to meditate any more than we have to learn how to concentrate. What we do have to learn is how to meditate constructively. We first learn to direct the creative process at work in our lives. Our careful observation will show us that we, ourselves, create all our joys and successes as well as our failures and unhappy states. Sometimes the time lapse between seed and fruit obstructs our recognition of this fact. Many of our present day creations had their origin in a meditative process originating years ago or even in a previous incarnation. One of the results of initiation into a true esoteric order is that our creative powers are stimulated so that the seeds we plant in the garden of subconsciousness come to fruition more quickly and abundantly. Thus the initiate may see the connection between the seeds (his images and reactions) and the fruits (circumstances, whether pleasant or painful) in his life.

We train in the use of meditation by choosing a focus that is interesting and can be easily expressed as a pictorial image. Don't choose an abstract idea as your focus until your skill has developed. To attempt to concentrate on abstract concepts in the primary phases can lead to discouragement and confusion.

The method favored by the Fraternity of the Hidden Light is to use the symbolic pictures of the Tarot to learn concentration. These pictorial symbols represent definite aspects of consciousness that we all possess in latent form. Proper use of the Tarot will aid us in developing such hidden powers. Adepts who understood these forces of consciousness as tools for training and balancing the personality created the Tarot.

To reiterate, in the course of the meditative process, concentration on delineated subjects causes subconsciousness to scan for related ideas that are presented to self-consciousness. Those ideas that are appropriate to the chosen goal are energized by our interest. Consciousness identifies and controls hidden forces by means of images. If you can understand these principles, you will have comprehended the meditative state and you will see the necessity for using this power in constructive imagery only.

Initiates will reach a stage where they can and should hold their minds and hearts in the meditative state almost continuously, scanning for the awareness of the truth behind every appearance that presents itself to them in their environment. This exalted state of constant meditation requires two things from the aspirant, serenity and efficiency. Of the two, the most important is serenity. By serenity we do not mean the outer appearance, but a true inward calm. Without this calm the inner work cannot be done. In the western Mysteries, we do not escape to a mountaintop retreat in order to avoid the unsettling pressures of our daily lives. We train to achieve sufficient thought control to be able to maintain our inner equilibrium even while dealing with the responsibilities of the outer world. Your practice with meditation on the Tarot Keys will aid in your development of this control and the images of the Tarot themselves will help you to realize your unity with the True Self at the center. From that central vantage point, the frustrations, conflicts, and ambitions of the personality level seem much less important. As a metaphor, think of how a loving and patient parent tenderly views a young child's struggles for growth. The parent knows the broken balloon, which seems so tragic to the child, will soon be forgotten. She also knows that the feelings of inadequacy that are so painful to the child will be the stimulus for growth. Similarly, our Higher Self, able to see the long-term picture, is not unsettled by these tempests, which appear so important to the personality's limited perception.

Efficiency is necessary in order to maintain serenity. Those who would seek to "sacrifice" their proper responsibilities to family and community in order to devote all of their efforts to their own growth are deluding themselves. Not only must the legitimate responsibilities of our daily lives be met, but met so efficiently that sufficient resources of time, energy and material needs are still available for the inner work - all this and maintain serenity too. It is very helpful to remember the traditional advice to an initiate, "I will look upon every circumstance as a direct dealing of God with my soul."

Chapter 37
Patanjali's Flow

The ancient yogi sage Patanjali defined meditation as, "an unbroken flow of knowledge in a particular object." This type of sustained dwelling on one central idea has definite physical consequences. The stillness required helps attune the body rhythm to the greater rhythm of the macrocosm. The seven interior centers, called chakras by the yogis and inner holy planets or metals by the alchemists, are activated and their balance and synchronization is aided by concentrated thought on appropriate images.

At first we have to persevere in establishing a regular habit of meditation. The subconscious mind is a creature of habit. Once regular practice of meditation is in place, the inertia of the subconscious mind, at first a source of resistance, becomes a factor in maintaining the routine. "We shall be as uneasy and discomforted if we miss our meditation-time as if we miss a meal" (Dion Fortune. 2000. *Aspects of Occultism.* Newburyport, MA: Red Wheel Weiser).

Individual preference determines the proper time of the day to devote to meditation. However, we recommend this practice be done in the morning, immediately after dressing, but before breakfast. The absence of food facilitates the process and the time spent in cleaning and dressing lets us become fully alert so that we don't drift back to sleep. The mind fresh from sleep and still free from the concerns of the day is ready for the examination of the inner life. We want to emphasize that there is no better investment one can make towards spiritual development and the path of initiation than this half-hour of sacrificed sleep.

Many students have attempted to meditate while lying in bed, before getting up, only to find that they often fall back to sleep. Soon this can become a conditioned response: whenever they start to meditate, they fall asleep! We do not recommend this practice. However, it is a very good practice to turn the thoughts to invocation of the Higher Self for a few moments immediately upon awakening. Such an invocation, while the threshold of the conscious mind is lowered, is extremely potent. Soon the habit will be established and upon awakening you will find you are already subconsciously performing the invocation. The following examples are from "The Threshold" course for probationers.

Lord of Life, enthroned in my heart, look through my eyes, teach with my voice, heal with my hands today. Help me to know that I am one with Thee.

Or

Come Thou Bright and Eternal One, Who art my Own True Self. Take charge of this personality and guide me through service into the Light of GOD.

Chapter 38
The Power of Symbol in Ritual

With the recent popularity of works by the late Joseph Campbell as well as those by various members of the Jungian school, the psychological basis of ritual has been clearly demonstrated. This should not be taken to mean that spirituality is merely a phenomenon of the psyche. As has been pointed out repeatedly in the writings of such authors as Gareth Knight, W. G. Gray, Dion Fortune and Dolores Ashcroft-Nowicki, there are objective inner dimensions. And in those dimensions, usually referred to as the Inner Planes of Consciousness, there exists entities that are quite independent of the human psyche.

The process of conditioning is very important in the Western Mysteries. When its techniques have been mastered, an initiate can evoke a specific state of consciousness by visualizing or simply looking at a corresponding symbol with intent. But it is not only trained initiates who are affected by this process. In all spiritually minded people, this conditioning results in an attitude of love mingled with awe; in the ignorant it results in an attitude of awe mixed with superstitious fear. Dion Fortune gives the opinion that only the "enlightened skeptic" is free of this conditioning. But many studies have indicated that unless these individuals have thoroughly "re-conditioned" themselves to another, more "enlightened" set of symbols, they will, in a crisis, revert back to their childhood training. This is the "there is no such thing as an atheist in a foxhole" phenomenon.

These symbols and mythological systems, known since early childhood, constitute an extremely important part of our cultural treasure. They are keys that unlock the door of our racial or ethnic egregore and admit us to the group mind of our native tradition. These symbols are elucidated during the course of initiation into the esoteric systems. I can personally attest that, no matter how much I may love "New Age" music, it is still the hymns of my childhood that strike a responsive chord in my soul and provide me with those "epiphany" moments of mystical elation. "No mystical or philosophical explanation, however profound or satisfying to the intellect, can replace early associations," Dion Fortune tells us. It is for this reason that spiritual seekers of the West have such a hard time in fully integrating into an initiatory school of the Eastern Tradition. They lack the keys in their psyche necessary to unlock the door and gain full acceptance into the soul levels of these otherwise valid training systems.

As I mentioned earlier, it is to make this contact of power more easily accessible that most valid esoteric fraternities encourage, and in some cases require, their students to familiarize themselves with these images by immersing themselves in the study of myths, fairy tales, the holy books, etc. These symbols penetrate deeply, often times bypassing the conscious mind. When a child is instructed in the tenets of his faith, what is really occurring is a conditioning process of his or her reflexes to the sacred symbols. The fine details or theology are lost upon him. But the allegories, legends and parables find root because they are based upon pictures and symbols, and symbolic consciousness develops before we learn to think in words. Consequently, our sense of the symbolic is developed and efficient at an age when "word thinking" is rudimentary. The sacred picture and the sacred image are far more potent than the illuminated text.

The process of ritual initiation reconditions the individual psyche to the sacred symbols. In the Mysteries, the simple dramatic, sacred stories, whether historical or mythic, are given a mystical interpretation. This was true in the Egyptian mysteries, in the Eleusinian system (as in the myth of Demeter, Hades and Persephone) as well as in the story of C. R., known from the Rosicrucian tradition. All of these make their primary impact via the conditioned response to the symbols. A heightened metaphysical, mystical explanation is then provided. This is the strong meat of the teaching for those who are prepared; for those who grew initially on milk, appropriate when they were just babes.

The transforming process, which is the purpose of initiation, rests upon this early conditioning. In order to make the most dramatic impact upon the candidate's consciousness, they are staged in the most evocative and impressive of settings. They are kept secret so that the candidate cannot anticipate the experience and thereby lessen its impact. By this process, a symbol presented with a new mystical interpretation plants a potent suggestion deep into the subconscious of the initiate.

The consciousness of the candidate has been sensitized through a long period of preparation and examination. Then, he is hoodwinked and brought into an atmosphere full of evocative mystery. Strange odors of incense are sensed. Often the lighting of the hall is arranged to let his imagination heighten all images. Sonorous intonations are sounded and questions that require an immediate and deep probing of his motivation are asked. Suddenly, the blindfold is removed and the candidate sees before him an impressive scene, calculated to have the greatest impact upon his consciousness. The officers and members are all trained initiates engaged in creating, through their combined concentration, a suggestion or image that impresses the imagination of the candidate. Because of his preparation, sensitivity and conditioning, the influence of the lodge floods through to him. A link is formed under the ritualistic conditions of intense emotional arousal. Forever after, the phrases, symbols and signs associated with this experience will evoke from the candidate a powerful and emotional sense of this link and a shift of consciousness similar to the one he first experienced at his initiation. It is not uncommon for an initiate, merely by giving the "sign" and uttering the "word," to attune his consciousness to that aspect of power represented by the corresponding grade of initiation. Thus, the consciousness of the candidate is impressed, because of his preparation, sensitivity and through the agency of his own imagination as well as the psychic influence of the group mind, channeled through the combined mental influence of the lodge.

This effect is further increased in intensity by the activities following the initiation. The initiate is directed in the weeks to come to take the symbols to which he has been linked and conditioned and to make them the focus for his daily meditations. Further, he takes the scheme of the ceremony as a whole and applies its symbolism to the awakening of the higher consciousness.

There are some symbols that embody archetypal power. Certain of these are so powerful that they "take charge" when they are formulated by anyone who is at all sensitive. This is one of the reasons for the phenomenon referred to as a thought-form. When highly trained minds use a symbol as the focus for meditative and ritual work for long periods of time, a tremendous amount of power becomes focused around them. These symbols are still used by adepts to transform consciousness so that it reaches its full potential.

These symbols are the carefully guarded secrets of the esoteric fraternities. Through these, the initiates makes contact with the Inner School. These Masters are continuously broadcasting, but it is by use of these contact symbols that we may "tune in" to our especial inner partners.

In each degree or initiatory grade there is a "word" and a "grade sign." These words and symbols key the consciousness to the memory and the current of energy, active in the initiatory experience. It is through the trained, emotionally charged imagination that this experience may be made use of. And, as one adept once wrote "…the mind, concentrated and exalted by ceremonial can do things of which it is normally incapable."

Chapter 39
The Four Maxims

It should be obvious to the reader by now that when we "work a ritual" we are building a pattern in the "mind-stuff" that allows for an inflow of dynamic, conscious energy. This flow occurs from the archetypal centers of Briah, through Yetzirah, and if successful, affects manifestation in Assiah.

Magic has traditionally been defined in the works of Aleister Crowley as "changes in conformance to Will." Dion Fortune modified this by adding that the "changes" were changes in "consciousness." The difference is irrelevant since all changes are preceded or caused by changes in consciousness. Gareth Knight recently defined it as "the skilled and objective use of the imagination both as the organ of perception and expression..." This is, in every way, a superior definition for it points out the relationship between the inner and outer worlds.

The key to effective magical ceremony lies in prior conditioning of the consciousness to the symbols employed. Ritual creates a multisensory suggestion that leads to prolonged concentration. This activity aligns the inner and outer consciousness, allowing a free-flowing power pathway that connects the objective consciousness in the world of Assiah with the relevant archetype in Briah.

When working with the powerful symbols and potencies of ritual, it is important to remember the maxims of Hermes. Hermes taught four words that are critical in carrying out any effective ceremony: "Know, Will, Dare, and Be Silent."

To Know

"Know" and "Knowledge" in Hebrew is "Da'ath." This term is connected in the Qabalah with the invisible quasi-sephirah that is situated at the conjunction of the 13th Path of Gimel and the 14th Path of Daleth. This intersection is in the midst of the Great Abyss. One of its symbols is the "Empty Room" and recalls the Chaldean Oracle's passage that states, "I am the only being in an abyss of darkness…"

In all of these mystical attributions lies the central idea of linking or "uniting." The symbol of the empty room or shrine is a place where human and Divine consciousness meet. The 14th path of Daleth reinforces this uniting in that it links the male archetype represented by Chokmah with the Great Mother in Binah, transforming the "Dark Sterile Mother 'Amah'" into the "Bright Fertile Mother 'Aimah'" by the addition of the seed letter, Yod. And, finally, the fact that Da'ath is located on the middle of the 13th path, which carries the title of "the Uniting Intelligence," reinforces these associations with union.

Of course, the first injunction is to "know" why you are doing what you are doing. As we have pointed out, the selection of an "intention" cannot be over emphasized. All other decisions flow from it. This is the goal of the ritual and it focuses and organizes our efforts – our energy. It deserves a great deal of reflection and meditation. Besides the benefits already mentioned, it also initiates the symbolic associations or chains of consciousness in relation to this focus. It calls these constellations nearer to the surface so that they can be stimulated by the activities of the ceremony.

Aleister Crowley stated that Da'ath could be considered to exist on an altogether different plane than the rest of the sephiroth. This is a useful image for understanding Da'ath. I would suggest, however, that its function is best revealed by its position on the Tree. Traditionally, as we have pointed out, it is located at the conjunction (and balance point) of the 13th and 14th paths. (See Figure Five).

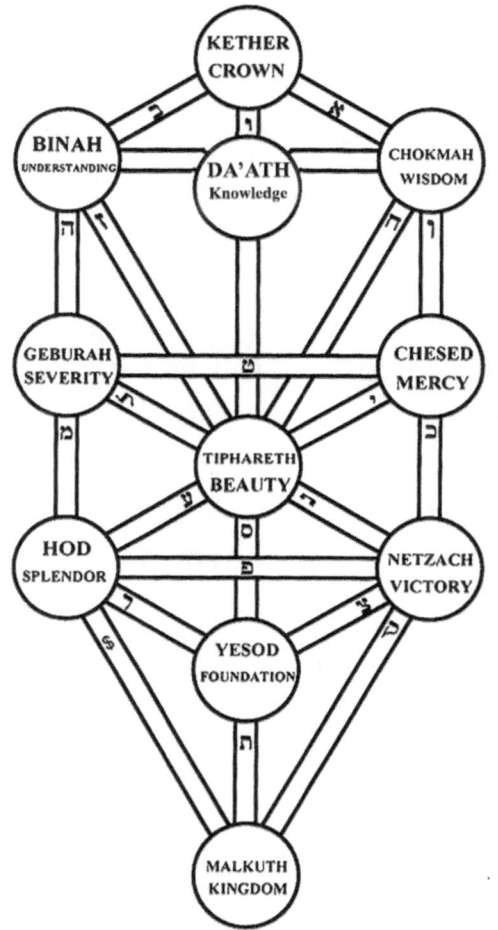

Figure Five

The 14th Path, assigned to the Hebrew letter Daleth is the highest of the reciprocal paths, also known as the "Paths of Equilibrium." The other two being the 19th Path of Teth and the 27th Path of Peh. These three reciprocal paths are so-called because the energy is said to flow equally in both directions. These paths share an interesting relationship that is revealed when their corresponding Tarot symbols are examined. The 16th Key, "The Tower" is attributed to the 27th path; Key 8, "Strength," is attributed to the 19th path; and, finally the 14th path is connected with Key 3, "The Empress."

These horizontal paths all deal with the mysterious matter of polarity. The 27th path is associated with the planet Mars. Mars is the term used in the Western Mysteries for what in the Eastern Mysteries would be associated with Tantra and Kundalini. Tantra is the Yoga of Sex. The Kundalini is that fiery psycho-neuro energy stored at the Sacral Chakra at the base of the spine. Examination of the diagram of "Adam Kadmon," or "The Grand Man," illustrated on the frontispiece of this volume, suggests this.

This mysterious force functions in all creative activities as well as in war! With Key 16, we see it primarily in its destructive aspect. However, its association with the planet Mars and with the area of the genitals on the figure of Adam Kadmon, suggests a focus on the sex drive in this instance.

On the 19th path, we see this same energy manifesting as the power of will. This aspect of will is discussed in more detail later on, but it is important to note now how it manifests in Key 8. A universal law states that all consciousness below the level of the human conscious mind is unfailingly amenable to suggestions originating at that human level. The woman symbolizes creative imagination, taming the lion, which indicates the animal nature, the subconsciousness, and the Mars energy. It is important to note that the woman uses a garland of roses to accomplish this. The rose, a symbol of love and the desire force, when woven into a garland, represents directed or trained desire. Here is a fundamental and profound key to magic.

This brings us to the reciprocal path that helps define Da'ath's position on the middle pillar. The 14th path of the letter Daleth links the sphere of Chokmah, assigned to God as the Divine Father with the sephirah Binah, attributed to God as the Divine Mother (See Figure Five).

In the Qabalah, Binah, as we have mentioned, has two attributions, "Amah" and "Aimah." Amah represents that "dark, terrible and sterile mother." This is somewhat analogous to the Hindu "Kali." In cosmology it represents the dark, cold vastness of the Void before the "Big Bang" exploded.

The second role assigned to Binah is that of Aimah the "bright, fertile Mother," the equivalent of the many earth goddesses, like Ceres or Demeter, for example. Remember what has been said previously about the Hebrew alphabet being hieroglyphic as well as phonetic. Then consider that what transforms Amah (אמה) into Aimah, (אימה) is the insertion of the letter Yod, (י), especially assigned to Chokmah. The shape of the Yod is said to symbolize the male seed! When the

Divine Feminine is "seeded" by the Cosmic Father, She is transformed into the "Bright, Fertile Queen of Heaven." The path of Daleth symbolizes the path where this occurs. Daleth is the word for "door" or "portal" and is considered among Qabalists as being a euphemism for the womb, this being the gateway to life. So, on this path, we see both the symbols of the "seed" and the "womb." Once again, we see the symbol of "union" in connection with the location of the sephirah whose name means "Knowledge."

Thus, the first injunction of Hermes is to become One or link with the Divine. This is supported by the command given to initiates to always invoke the Highest. By doing this supremely important act, we move our ceremonial from "Thaumaturgy" (Miracle or Magic-Working) to "Theurgy" (God-Working), and thus become channels for the Divine. With this link firmly established in consciousness, at least symbolically, we move to the second maxim.

To Will

The question of "free will" is one that has alternately fascinated or plagued historians of philosophy for centuries. From interpretations of "Do what Thou wilt shall be the whole of the Law!" to "Not my will but Thine be done." The range is wide – even among initiates. The position one takes hinges upon the interpretation of who "Thou" is and what is exactly meant by the word "Will."

In defense of Mr. Crowley, when he issued the injunction that is revered to this day by thousands of his followers, called Thelemites, he was not advocating the license to do anything you wish! The "Thou" in his statement was used in the Qabalistic sense where Thou or "Ateh" in Hebrew is assigned to the Primal Will attributed to the sephirah Kether. Thus he was in complete agreement with the words attributed to Jesus in the garden when he said, "Not my will but Thine be done."

In many of the psychic, metaphysical and astrological magazines we see advertisements for courses, seminars and books for developing "Will Power." Yet, in a communication from the "Inner Plane Adept" of the Fraternity of the Hidden Light, it is explained to us that "free will" below the level of the Individuality in Tiphareth is a fallacy. At the levels of personality and subconsciousness, all decisions are, by and large, a stimulus/response mechanism. Sometimes these are very complex, but should not be considered the exercise of free will. Before we discourage the reader too much we should point out that the same source emphasized that when we align our personal "will" with the Cosmic Will emanating from levels higher or deeper than the personality, it is, in fact, completely free. "Not my will..."

Will, as understood by initiates, is not personal, but rather a Cosmic potency. This Will is the source of our determinations, etc. and we function most effectively when we align with it.

"To Will" commands the ceremonialist to provide focus and direction for the Universal Will Power, pouring continuously through him.

This is accomplished by concentration and imagination. Observe the posture of "The Hermit," the Tarot trump assigned to the Qabalistic "Intelligence of Will." Here is a picture of the adept in the midst of directing this force, through imagery, to achieve his (and by identification) God's purpose. It points out that for the adept ritualist, an entire ritual may be performed internally. However, for most practitioners, the "props" of a temple and associated paraphernalia are helpful. In fact, the acts of selecting, constructing or collecting the ritual objects can be a magical act in themselves. However, this can reach a point of diminishing return, as we shall discuss in the next section.

To Dare

I once knew an initiate who spent endless hours revising the format of his printed ritual, drawing elaborate diagrams, collecting beautiful ritual tools and robes. The problem was that I never saw or heard of him ever doing any rituals with them! In the Tradition we hear a lot about the "arm-chair magician." This is the individual who reads and prepares, reads and prepares and then does still more reading and preparing but all of his "magic" is stillborn. The "paralysis of analysis" has taken root. He never moves from preparation to execution. True, for an experienced practitioner the ritual can be performed totally in the mind. <u>But it must be performed</u>!

Another colleague of mine once remarked to me about magic that, "I would rather attempt something and get my tail feathers singed through an error than to play it safe and do nothing, risk nothing and thereby gain nothing!" She followed up by saying, "At least with singed feathers you are convinced of the reality of the inner forces and this attitude will help you make much more progress than immeasurable hours of theorizing."

It all comes down to the fact, that to be successful in ceremonial we must complete the circuit of power. We must have the courage (tempered with discrimination of course) to give some form of physical expression to our patterns of consciousness. We must assume a bold confident attitude of mind. Faint, half doubting expressions simply will not work.

We must dare to be an effective magical ritualist.

To Keep Silent

I once, while on a television show, commented about the phenomenon of the "proselytizer." This is an individual who has newly discovered the mysteries and riches of the "esoteric path." We have probably all met this type. They are the ones whose enthusiasm is so fired up about the truly great treasure they have found that they tell everyone who they think may be interested. Then, they tell all those who they think might be sympathetic. Then, they proceed to tell all those who are disinterested or unsympathetic and perhaps even hostile!

Consider the reactions of all those who, the "newborn" has enthusiastically but, perhaps indiscriminately, attempted to rally. Jealousy? Aggression? When we realize the power of thought we realize that even thoughts from friends may impede our goals. But it goes even deeper than that. When we consider something sacred, we hold it closely and well-protected in our minds. We accomplish this with silence. Silence conserves and even builds power. Of the four maxims, silence is the most difficult and yet the most important. Hence it is given last. When a farmer plants a seed he doesn't dig it up every day to see how it is growing! We don't have to "talk" our goals into manifestation. We plant the seed through the medium of our ceremony and rest with confidence that it will be accomplished.

Chapter 40
The Initiation of Fire

The Initiation of Fire is associated with the Latin title, "Philosophus" which means "one who loves wisdom." It is the highest grade of the First Order and completes the attunements of the personality in the "Lesser Mysteries." It is referred to the sephirah "Netzach" which means "Victory." It is in Netzach, therefore, that the final victory of the work of transformation takes place.

We have written elsewhere about the critical nature of our concept of the desire force. Desire is the key that will open the temple of transmutation of consciousness. Through it, we will complete the Great Work. It is referred to the metal copper, concerning which the alchemical text the "Turba Philosophorum" instructs us "to wash until it is white and then make visible coins." To wash until white is to purify our personal desire until we see the link of it as a pure vehicle for the Divine Purpose seated in Kether. Then we make visible coins by manifesting this illumination in our daily thought, emotions and actions.

But to have sincere desire alone will prove to be inadequate. We never leave a grade when we move on to the next. Thus, to effect this transmutation we may marshal the realizations and skills that we have gained in the previous grades to form a perfect, whole instrument as the vehicle of illuminated consciousness.

"Enflame thyself with prayer!" is the counsel of the old writings. The necessity of getting outside ourselves till we feel the flaming descent of the Divine flowing through us in an ecstasy of spiritual transformation cannot be faked! This awareness that we are a channel for the "repairing of the worlds" leads us to the certain knowledge that the One Force, Substance and Consciousness are identical with what we, at our human level call Love. It is the power with which we unite in the Initiation of the Greater Mysteries. Thus we become "lovers of wisdom."

Philosophy, as any college freshman can tell you, deals with the ultimate questions. These are usually delineated as: "Who am I?" Why am I here?" Where am I going?" And, "What is my purpose?" These questions occupy all religions as well. Traditionally, Mystery Schools do not require their initiates to be members of any particular exoteric religion. They are encouraged to participate in the faith of their choice. However, without exception, all valid initiatory systems require their candidates to profess a belief in a Supreme Being. It is this belief that guides the initiate of this degree in the contemplation of these important questions.

The Mysteries of Eleusis declared, "I am a child of the earth, but my race is from the starry heavens." Thus it is stated in symbolic form that at the center of our being, we are divine. However it may appear to the contrary, we are an ever-evolving perfection, at one with the source of all perfection.

The "Pattern on the Trestle Board" states, "I am a center of expression for the Primal Will-to-Good, which eternally creates and sustains the universe." And again, "The Kingdom of Spirit is embodied in my flesh." These profound statements, received by Dr. Paul Foster Case during meditation, reaffirm that, at our essence, we are an extension of the one creating, supporting, transforming and redeeming power in the universe. When we recognize this, we will "lift all others unto ourselves," and will liberate and illuminate all the other kingdoms of which we have been made the guardians.

This "philosophy" is not a matter of conjecture. It is a record of verifiable experience, passed down to us by those Great Initiates who have gone before. It is from them that we have received the Tree of Life, the Tarot and the many other tools and disciplines that comprise the mystery schools of initiation. All that is necessary to make use of this wisdom is to develop the correct attitude so that we receive it.

Chapter 41
You've got to Have Heart!

One of the Masters of the Wisdom was once quoted as saying, "The intellect is a dull can opener with which to probe the secrets of the heart!"

Our deep consciousness, our magical world, is not really concerned with how smart we are if we don't communicate our ideas and our vision with imagination and passion. You've got to have heart! The path of initiation must be a balanced journey based upon the guiding stars of Power, Wisdom and Love. Wisdom, unless balanced by Love, becomes void of Power and devolves into an armchair hobby replacing the transformative work. It is like a cut flower arrangement. It may look impressive, but cut off from its roots and nourishment it will wither and die.

Emotion is the gas that powers the engine of aspiration. If we don't care enough or if we have deliberately cut ourselves off from our passion, then we separate ourselves from our power. Our subconsciousness interprets this as a lack of commitment and priority and produces results to fulfill this image. The path to illumination is not just a mind game. It is a continual purification of our image patterns by our emotionally charged, persistent vigilance.

Those who have studied the history of the Qabalistic movement of the "Chasidim" and their founder, The Baal Shem Tov, know that this Qabalistic adept would "lose himself in ecstasy." And in an ancient ritual of Qabalistic magic known as "The Sacred Magic of Abra-Melin," the author exhorts the practitioner to "enflame thyself with prayer!" Followers of Wicca are taught to work themselves into an emotionally exalted state when raising a "cone of power."

The common key to these various techniques is ecstasy with the focus of desire as a gateway to the higher consciousness. Our passion charges our imagery and activates the energy paths that connect our manifest universe with the archetypal sources.

Contrast this to the meditative method, which in most schools of training in the West is used to balance the ceremonial path. In meditation we seek to quiet and calm this energy. For this reason both should be used to provide a balanced, rounded development.

Anyone who has entered esoteric training for any period of time knows that, periodically, they will run into "dry periods." These are the times when their studies seem to bring forth little success. It is during these periods when the aspirant asks himself or herself whether it is really worthwhile to continue their studies. They ask themselves, "Am I in the right school?" Experienced students will recognize this as a manifestation of a cycle. Even for them it will require self-discipline to maintain the regimen necessary to continue progressing in their studies. Their passion will seem to have deserted them and to have "dried up."

It is during these barren periods that some students have found value in occult, mystical or fantasy fiction. Some of these stories, when written by persons with an initiated background, can provide knowledge as well as entertain. But even those that are just "good reads" can provide inspiration and fire the imagination. These books and stories are like oases in the middle of the desert at these dry times. They enable us to persevere and push to a newer and perhaps higher realization! They can turn a breakdown experience into one of breakthrough! Thus, I recommend that students stay on the lookout for good selections from among these types of works. They provide food for the imagination. In general, I read at least one piece of fiction for every two non-fiction works when I am doing research.

Chapter 42
To Purify, to Consecrate, to make Holy

Purification

The term "purification" comes from the Latin word "purificare," to make pure. As it refers to ritual, it does not particularly carry the moralistic meanings often associated with it. Rather, it is more closely related to the meaning of the word when used chemically as, for example, in the terms "distilled water" or "absolute alcohol" or "99 and 9/10% pure." In other words, free from adulteration or contamination.

The act of purification aids us in breaking the association with any extraneous mental or etheric connections with other objects, areas or work we are simultaneously involved with. This occurs on the mental level as well as the material. It is, in essence, a type of "Banishing."

The rite of "lustral purification" is one of the oldest of ceremonies. It is traditionally accomplished by the act of sprinkling water that has been especially blessed for this purpose. The type of blessing is largely dictated by choice or custom. In many fraternities a very small amount of salt is placed in the water prior to its use. Adding salt to the water, if performed with serious intent, transforms the liquid into "Holy Water." Remember it is the intent backed by the desire force that accomplishes this transformation. When the salt is added to the water, we have an interaction of the two "passive" elements, Water and Earth. Thus, it is the passive elements that are used as the vehicle to purify. Symbolically, they are assigned to the Qabalistic worlds of Briah (Water) and Assiah (Earth).

Magic, to a very large extent, concerns purifying the power paths extending from the Archetypes in Briah through the symbolic chains of Yetzirah to finally manifest in the desired manner in Assiah. Thus, it is imperative to cleanse the subconscious links of any erroneous patterns to the greatest extent possible. When we purify, we use the energy symbolized by the element of water, the "mind-stuff." This flowing energy is referred to in the old alchemical texts as the "water that does not wet the hand." It responds readily to the imprint of the image-making powers of the creative imagination.

Consecration

Whereas the "passive" elements are normally used for purification, in consecration, the active elements are used. The term comes from the Latin con "with," and sacre "sacredness" or "holiness." When we consecrate we do it with holiness. A consecrated object or action is done with intent to set it apart for holy or sacred purposes.

The element of Fire is attributed to the holy letter "Shin" (c) in Qabalah. The other active element is Air, attributed to the letter "Aleph" (a). There is a close connection in the symbolism surrounding these two letters.

Indeed, when Eliphas Levi published the Hebrew alphabet attributions for the Tarot trumps in the nineteenth century, he employed a "blind" by exchanging the two trumps belonging to these letters.

Shin is attributed to Fire. Aleph, besides being assigned to the element of Air, also carries the title, "The Fiery Intelligence." Fire has always been associated with the "Holy Spirit." There are numerous examples in the Bible that illustrate this, the most obvious being the events surrounding Pentecost in the Book of Acts.

Additionally, Fire is the transforming element. In a mystical sense, we have only to recollect that offerings were many times burnt upon an altar. Thus, when we consecrate, we align ourselves with this divine power. It is this power, flowing through us, that accomplishes the sanctifying process.

As purification is closely aligned to "banishing," consecration is similar to "invoking." It is of the utmost importance when performing either of these ceremonial acts to reinforce them with appropriate imagery. Remember, the outward act is to confirm and reinforce an inner change in consciousness.

What follows is a guided imagery exercise that I have used many times in training students and in our public workshops. Without fail, in every case, when questioned both before and after, the audience easily felt the difference. The following imagery may be of help with purification:

You are standing on the sacred plain immediately in front of the Great Temple of the Sun on the island of Ruta in Ancient Atlantis. It is in the early hours just before sunrise. You face east toward the Great Golden Gates awaiting the first rays of dawn to strike the huge pylons. All around you are your brothers and sisters of the Sacred Clan, priests and priestesses all. Out of all of these you have been selected to perform one of the most ancient and most honored of all ceremonial acts --- The Dawn Purification.

You are dressed in the sleeveless, knee length white robe and you hold the silver chalice filled with the sacred, lustral water. As the first rays of the sun strikes the huge gateposts, you dip your right hand into the water and sprinkle towards the rising sun. With power, your voice vibrantly rings forth: "I purify by Water!" In your eye of vision you see the mighty waves of the Astral Ocean crashing forth to remove any impurity or contamination. You turn clockwise and complete the action for the other three directions before returning to your original position and lifting the chalice in salute to the rising sun, physical symbol of the Eternal Spiritual Light!"

We can, of course, easily adapt this type of visualization to fit other ritualistic acts, such as consecration. The student should use the principles illustrated and create their own images, those that are meaningful to them personally and fit the system they are using.

Warding

While "Warding" is not synonymous with "Banishing," they are closely related.

There seems to be some confusion as to the effect of a banishing ritual. The most famous is, of course, the so-called "Lesser Banishing Ritual of the Pentagram." First, it should be noted that the effective use of any of the elemental rituals of banishing, such as the "LBRP," is directly related to the operator and to their attainment of the corresponding grade. I know this flies in the face of many prominent published opinions, but an unbiased observation made within esoteric orders and lodges for well over 50 years (and longer, if accounts of the previous generation of initiates are considered) back this point of view.

Secondly, there is a popular misconception that banishing is aggressive in nature; that "we chase away the beasties" when we banish. This error is probably derived from the old grimoires or medieval magic manuals that have "licenses to depart" included in them. Some writers state that the effects of banishing are perceived as a "sterile, surgically antiseptic, barren atmosphere." I would suggest that this effect may be in the nature of a self-fulfilling prophecy. That is, they expect it and their consciousness complies. It has not been the experience of the author or of his associates in his particular Order.

I was taught, rather, that banishing has the effect of tuning the vibrations of perception to a more balanced, more equilibrated and more positive frequency. Therefore, any manifestations not consistent with these vibratory channels are excluded, much as if a channel has been changed on a television or radio. It will be noted that this later interpretation could also function as a "Pygmalion effect." However, it avoids the delusion of "separation" much more effectively.

Warding is a traditional term for placing symbolic seals for the purpose of rendering a given area of working invulnerable to inharmonious influences. It certainly involves banishing, but usually, consecration as well.

Examples can be found in certain churches and cemeteries. However, the best examples are found in occult fiction. Even though these are fictional accounts, the descriptions of the effects of the warding are essentially accurate. Two first class examples may be found in Dion Fortune's *The Secrets of Doctor Taverner*, in the episodes "The Death Hound" and "Blood Lust," where she describes the effects of warding as producing a "psychic bell-jar." Another good example is found in Katherine Kurtz's *Deryni* series. I encourage interested students to read these stories.

A properly warded area provides a secure working place free from distractions and inharmonious influences. This process also allows for the buildup and containment of beneficial energies to accumulate over a period of time. This effect can be readily observed in such places of power as Chartres Cathedral, Rosslyn Chapel, Saint Michael's Tor, the Hsi Lai Buddhist temple near Los Angeles and others. In a sense, these, and places like them, have become huge walk-in talismans, bestowing a sacred feeling on any receptive person who enters.

This effect can be greatly extended if a suitable, physical object can be used as a focus. Relics in churches are used for this purpose. In the Fraternity of the Hidden Light, mental imagery is reinforced by certain permanently placed objects known as "deposits." Their use is explained in a ritual known as the "Erection of the Wards Major."

I have personally observed people who were inharmonious with the given purpose of a temple or other location refuse to enter where these wards had been set. When questioned, they answered that they simply could not enter these environs.

Chapter 43
The Full Armor

Many times, consecrated regalia, implements, etc., when used over an extended period of time for dedicated purposes alone, will become "charged" with a highly powerful, subtle energy. We should not, however, fall onto the superstitious trap of thinking that any of these items inherently contain "magical power" in or of themselves. There is no magic without a magician. A talisman can have terrific magical power, but the magician who will later use it must consecrate it. However, it may be admitted that certain items take upon themselves a charge that can be picked up by anyone sufficiently sensitive who comes into contact with them. The famous "Hope Diamond" is an example of this. But on the whole, the imprint of a highly emotional charge must be accomplished. This is because all of the items that we are about to talk about owe their efficiency to the links made in the ritualist's consciousness between the object and the archetype. Therefore, the mind of the initiate should be conditioned to each tool or piece of regalia. There should be a thorough knowledge of its symbolism as well as a precise, disciplined formula for the activation and deactivation (opening or closing our consciousness) to the effect or the potency of the symbol.

What follows is a partial explanation of the symbolism of a selection of certain regalia together with a suggested "Vesting and Divesting Prayer." These are provided as examples for the illustration of the principles involved.

The Shoes

The Shoes or Sandals represent the dedicated and consecrated intention to walk in the way of the sacred as an initiate and priest or priestess of the Mysteries.

In some fraternities, such as in the Hermetic Order of the Golden Dawn, these were colored red to represent the "fire of zealous dedication," or gold in their second order, to represent the "purified gold of higher consciousness." In other fraternities, they are represented as white to symbolize the "pure intention to travel in the way of light." In yet another case, no shoes whatsoever are worn. The initiates in this group believes in the Biblical admonition, "Take thy shoes from off thy feet for thou dost stand on holy ground."

The desire and dedication to pursue the studies and disciplines of the Western Mysteries is often referred to as "Being on the Path" or "The Path of Return," and initiates are often referred to as "travelers," "journeymen," "pilgrims" or "wayfarers." So, the reminder to our consciousness that we have consecrated ourselves to walk the way of the sacred path is important and ever present.

Vesting Prayer for Shoes

Oh Divine Spirit, let these shoes remind me of my

Dedication to walk in the light. Let it remind me
That I was called to serve all life. Amen.

<u>Divesting</u>

As I remove these sacred sandals from my feet
Let the memory of my dedication remain with
Me in my daily walk. Amen.

In some fraternities, mention is made of the "silver sandals" and "golden sandals" and, in at least one instance, I've seen actual shoes colored in this manner worn in certain grades.

The silver sandals refer to those who have successfully "walked between the worlds," that is, have completed certain visionary experiences commonly known in the tradition as "pathworkings." This is not the daydreaming fantasy flights as popular books and fiction would have us believe. It is a thorough, systematic exploration of the inner realms. I have included two examples of pathworkings taken from our course "The Path of Return" in the appendixes of this book as examples.

The "golden shoes" represent a lofty spiritual attainment. I agree with my friend and colleague Dolores Ashcroft-Nowicki who once wrote, "There are few who can claim the right to wear those shoes!"

The Inner Robe of Glory

The Inner Robe represents two things: The individual's status as an initiate (hence it is usually the same color for all members of a lodge or fraternity); and the spiritual nature of the individual. Thus, many times it is white as it was in the Second or Inner Order of the Golden Dawn.

This white color serves also to link in consciousness the Primal Will in Kether to the initiate. Also, it is a reminder that each of us, at our inner level, is the "Eternal Virgin, forever pure and undefiled." This is a useful aid to counteract the centuries of accumulated nonsense about the so-called "sinful" nature. Initiates would do well to remember that they are a Divine creation! "My race is from the starry heavens," rather than feeling unjustified and unworthy. We should be focusing our dynamic image building power on "Original Godliness" and "Original Blessing," instead of "Original Sin." The following prayer helps us align our consciousness to these ideas:

Vesting Prayer

I don the seamless robe of Adonai! By this action I align myself as an instrument of Thy Will, Lord (or Lady). Amen.

Divesting

I give thanks for your Guidance and Protection, Lord. Amen.

Why do we wear robes, garments that resemble a dress and were used in the Middle East, Greece and China? Obviously you can (and I have) performed ceremonial in everyday clothes. I have seen a fraternal organization perform their rituals in Native American regalia. Freemasons wear tuxedos, suits or just everyday clothes. But they also wear aprons about which we will talk later.

The advantage of donning ritualistic clothes lies in the change of consciousness that occurs in the trained and conditioned mind. For this reason, ritual robes should never be worn for occasions not in keeping with their sacred intent. Failing to follow this simple rule can quickly dissipate the magnetism that builds up around them and the associative links in the mind. Do not follow the example of a Second Order member of the Golden Dawn who wore the robes of her grade to a fancy dress ball!

The Apron

The symbolism of the ritualistic apron descends to us from at least as far back as Ancient Egypt. For members of the modern esoteric schools of the West, most of the ideas associated with this ritualistic item probably come to us through Freemasonry. In that fraternity, great stress is placed upon the fact that it is an emblem of innocence and purity. It is traditionally made of lamb skin to connect it with the concept of sacrifice. But, just what is being sacrificed? Perhaps a hint is given when we consider what area of the body the apron covers. This is the generative organs and the

Mars Chakra. This symbolism refers to a raising or sublimation of the "Mars Force," sometimes called Kundalini, in dedication to the Great Work of Transmutation. This is further emphasized by the attribution of this part of the body, symbolically, to the zodiacal sign Scorpio, the so-called "night house of Mars." The attribution of lamb skin to the apron is a direct reference to the zodiacal sign Aries, the "day house of Mars." This sign is said to rule the frontal and upper parts of the brain. Here, for those who have ears to hear is a key symbolic statement. The work of transmutation involves the purifying and "lifting up" of the energy that is also used in reproduction from the genital area to awaken or activate those areas found in the upper and front sections of the brain. These organs of spiritual awareness are normally present in a most rudimentary state in the non-adept. Let us be clear, this symbolic relationship does not advocate any trickery dealing with the sex act. The energy we are speaking of concerns an internal residual energy left over and not used in most normal human beings.

In some Grand Lodge jurisdictions, the newly initiated Mason is instructed to wear his apron with the flap turned up to guard against soiling his clothing with "untempered mortar." Untempered mortar is a symbol for immature and selfish mental images. It is by control of images at the point of their creation that we effect the successful operation of this part of the Great Work.

Consider the Apron with the flap up. Here is a symbolic depiction of the principles under discussion. Note that we have a square, the geometrical symbol for Earth, and a triangle, the symbol of Fire. The Fire triangle surmounting the Earth symbol states emblematically that this force is sublimated or lifted up from its normal earthy expression to a more spiritual channel.

Notice also the similarity of this figure to the Pentagram in its proper upright position. In both of these figures the point of spirit is above or surmounts the four points assigned to the elemental nature. This depicts the truth; that the Spirit which is our true identity ("the I Am") is the ruler of our elemental world.

On construction jobs, a worker's apron usually has pockets or pouches to carry his working tools. In ceremonial aprons these "working tools" are usually represented by symbols depicted upon the front.

Whatever the design of this piece of regalia, the individual initiate should devote time to meditation on its symbolic significance.

Vesting Prayer

I don this Apron that I may become a builder
Of that Temple not made with hands, eternal
In the heavens. Amen.

Divesting

As I enter from labor to rest, may the
Symbolic truths this Apron represents
Guide me so that I may, with the Divine
Permission, complete my work!

The Stole

In all probability, the stole originated with the prayer shawls worn by devout Jews. Officially, however, it was the Emperor Constantine who proclaimed that priests of the early Christian church were given the right to wear the stole as a symbol of their office. Up to that time, it had been reserved for members of the Imperial Senate.

The stole has come to represent the "yoke" or obligation of the priesthood or ministry. It is generally bestowed upon a man or woman at the time of their ordination or consecration. Thus, it should not be worn by anyone who is not so obligated. I have seen certain members of fraternities who are not ordained wear them and I, personally, think this is symbolically incorrect. You might as well wear the wimple and vestments of a nun without having taken "orders."

Gareth Knight had the opinion that, in one sense, the stole might represent the outer pillars of the Tree of Life.

A variation of the stole is the Golden Dawn baldric or sash of the grades. In the G.D., this article of regalia was worn diagonally from shoulder to hip and bore upon its face the symbols of the grades and paths the individual initiate had attained. Anyone wishing to see this piece of regalia may refer to Israel Regardie's *The Golden Dawn*. As we vest with this item, either baldric or stole, as applicable, we should ever bear in mind that it represents a dedication to serve. Since this should always be the primary motivation in all of our ceremonies, I have not provided a sample vesting or divesting prayer. This is an intensely personal point that I leave to each ritualist.

The Girdle

The girdle or cincture is a stylized form of belt. In some traditions it is sacred to the Goddess. If it is colored red, it is said to be the belt of the initiate. It represents the magic circle of the cosmos, the circle "whose center is everywhere and circumference is nowhere." When a magician stands at the center of his circle of power, he affirms the truth that he possesses divine creative power. The fact is, we continually create our universe on a moment-to-moment basis. Those images that we energize with our desire force become the matrix, the framework for our manifestation. This is what is symbolized by the cincture or girdle of the ritualist.

Prayer of Vesting

I gird myself, oh Lord (or Lady) assuming the Armor of Light, standing boldly in the Truth of the
Recognition of my Divine Son/Daughtership. Amen.

Divesting

The Lord has declared that we are the inheritors
of the Kingdom. To us is given the riches of Abundance. Amen.

The Crown

Crowns and headgear, in general, have a long traditional place in ceremonial, but have almost disappeared in modern lodges.

In old texts we see references to mitres (like those worn by bishops) made of "virgin" or new parchment. Some rituals indicate the ceremonialist don a headpiece as is prescribed for the High Priest of the Jewish Tabernacle or Temple. Eliphas Levi entwined a garland of leaves in his hair! Some Golden Dawn groups still choose to wear the Egyptian style nemes. I have seen the use of full-blown crowns, some of very beautiful and symbolic workmanship. These ranged from the horned-crescent crown of a Wiccan High Priestess to those more Qabalistically oriented.

The crown refers to the idea of royalty, anointing and rulership. Qabalistically, it is related to the sephirah Kether, meaning "The Crown" and is assigned to the seat of the Yekhidah or "Indivisible One." As the ritualist places the crown upon his or her head, it is important to hold the image of aligning the personal will to that of the Divine.

Vesting Prayer for Crown

I offer myself as an instrument of Thy beneficent
Power, Wisdom and Love, oh Lord (or Lady) of the
Universe. Not my will but Thine be done! Amen.

Divesting Prayer

I give thanks oh Lord for the privilege of consciously acting as a channel for the manifestation of Thy Will. Amen.

The Lamen and the Personal Seal

The Lamen is a pendant or symbolic device that is usually worn suspended from a ribbon or chain around the neck. Normally, it hangs just over the heart. Sometimes, it represents the particular ritualistic office of the wearer as in Freemasonry and the "Talisman of Tzeleritas" that is worn by the Steward of the

Fraternity of the Hidden Light. At other times, it recognizes the particular aspect of consciousness being worked with in a ceremony. Or, it may depict a symbolic device that is common to a ritualist's group. Examples of this last case can be found in "The Cross of the Brethren," worn by certain early Rosicrucian groups.

The Lamen often represents the aspiration of the ritualist, "that which is laid upon their heart." In such a case, it can be unique to the individual.

An interesting piece of trivia related to the "seals" of the various Fraternities is that those related to the Rosicrucian Order (the Inner Plane one, not an external organization) often have the heptagon as a part of their seals. Those related to the "Hermetic Order" will often have octagons around their seals. Thelemic vehicles and Gnostic groups favor the vesica. Independent observation will confirm this.

The concept of a personal seal or symbol probably has its roots in the "Mark Mason's" degree of the York Rite of Freemasonry. During the course of this degree, the individual initiate selects a "mark" or unique symbol, usually designed by him, as an identifying sign.

This personal seal embodies the ritualist's ideal, that is, what he hopes to become and hopes to stand for. Although not well known, it is used in what is called "skrying" or "traveling in the Spirit Vision," "Pathworking" or "Lucid Dreaming." Anyone who has experience in this traveling, deep within the imagination, knows that it is customary to retrace his or her steps to the initial starting point when concluding the working. This ensures a complete integration of the visionary experience as well as making sure of a complete return or "earthing" of the energies. But, occasions may arise when there is an urgent need to terminate a skrying. This can cause panic and a nasty experience. A "traveler" can come back feeling dissociated, with the unsettling feeling of being both "here" and "there" at the same time. This occurs when the planes of consciousness lose their definition. In normal consciousness, the planes of awareness are discrete.

In the practice of certain spiritual exercises, the awareness of one level does not usually overlap with another. Such an overlap can be avoided by the use of a simple visionary technique. When the occasion for rapid withdrawal occurs, the skryer first visualizes a gateway, doorway or portal with their personal seal emblazoned over it on the lintel. Then, in imagination, he or she "steps through," turns, and then seals this doorway with a suitable banishing or warding gesture. They will then find themselves safely back in normal waking consciousness, in current time and space.

The Ring of Power

There is a story in Dion Fortune's, *The Secrets of Dr. Taverner*, that includes a confrontation between Taverner and a villain. Dr. Taverner makes a sign with his right hand and the villain, taken aback, leans forward and stares at the ring upon the Doctor's hand. He gasps in recognition and exclaims, "The Senior of Seven!" I remember when I read that story as a lad of fifteen, how it fired my imagination. The "Ring of Power!"

Later, during my training in the Fraternity, I discovered the more important, magical use of the ring, (besides scaring "bad guys" that is). It has to do with the assumption of what is known in the esoteric orders as the "Magical Personality."

We could compare our normal personality to a house built without any preconceived plan. When there was a need, we simply added a room. For example, without proper planning, often times we end up with the bathroom only accessible through a bedroom. In reference to the personality, when it comes time to invoke the high-tension powers of advanced magical work, it would be like attempting to build a second story upon an insufficient foundation. It simply would not stand the strain and the whole "house" might collapse altogether!

Thus, through a series of prolonged meditative exercises, lasting several months, if not years, initiates undertake to build an artificial personality. This personality, built in a deliberate and predetermined way, is used for magical and associated work only. It is built upon a balanced plan based upon the three major rays or aspects. These, as we have previously stated are Wisdom, Power and Love. This "Magical Personality" can handle the high energy of the esoteric practices of the Mystery Tradition much better than our normal "built-up-in-reaction-to-life-experiences" one.

The effect of repeated use of this magical consciousness will be that, bit-by-bit, it will reinforce and strengthen the everyday consciousness by providing a balanced template. Thus the Magical Personality is in the nature of a set of "training wheels" for adeptship. Be that as it may, we are taught a definite formula for "turning on" the artificial personality and for "turning it off" when doing formal work so that it will not intrude into everyday consciousness or vice versa.

The formula for assumption is very simple and straightforward and involves the Ring. In most of the esoteric fraternities the individual initiate is given a "motto" or magical name. This represents his or her highest aspirations. Usually, only the initiate and his initiator (and sometimes the other members of the lodge), know this name or formula. Only on extremely rare occasions is it publicized outside of the member's fraternity to the public. If a person is working solo, that is, is not within as lodge, they could adopt a name after due meditation on its import.

When assuming the Magical Personality, the aspirant very deliberately puts the ring on his finger and, together with a willed intention, assumes the personality by saying:

"I am _____ (whatever his motto is)."

When transitioning back to the mundane personality, the process is similar. The ring is taken off the finger with:

"I am _____(the everyday name)."

The Child of Earth
(A poem)

I am a Child of the Earth
But my Spirit is from the Starry Heavens!
I have been birthed from the Light
And have come to light the flame.
To see the Truth in each one's eyes
And know that we are one.

I call to those who have nurtured the Vision,
To those who felt the call,
To walk with the gift held tightly,
To heal all those who fall.

To walk the Path, to seek the Star,
To follow the Quest for no matter how long,
how far.
To light the flame within all they meet.
To celebrate the triumph of that
Which dwells at the heart!

Chapter 44
The Dweller on the Threshold

The transition from the experience of the Lesser Mysteries to those of the Greater Mysteries requires a period of adjustment and balancing. This is as it should be. For times of great and momentous change should be preceded by a term of reflection and anticipation. In our tradition this period is often referred to as "The Ordeal of the Portal." Here the initiate assumes the function of the god "Janus," looking back and assessing his journey thus far and gazing ahead, forward and upward to his goal of enlightenment. Most aspirants know that, at every moment, we stand upon a threshold of eternity, gazing at a future of unlimited possibilities and uncertain outcomes. But, as they should likewise realize, they can influence the alternatives of tomorrow by the images they consecrate today. At no time is this more evident than when they stand in the Portal.

This requires a ruthlessly honest self-assessment of their progress in the Lesser Mysteries by focusing on the present and analyzing situations and conditions that are causing pain and restriction. They begin by taking responsibility and then, by objective analysis, establishing the chain of causation. This brings them to the realization that the repercussions of the binding or limiting conditions are invariably the product of choices made as the result of the misapplication of the faculties of personality. This frees the aspirant to change the response in the future to similar conditions and become proactive rather than reflexive. The repeated selection of responses, more in harmony with the higher aspiration of the initiate, balances the temple of the personality. This is referred to, symbolically, as "establishing the dominion of the Spirit depicted as the Pentagram with the single point uppermost."

The four lower points refer to the elemental nature of human consciousness and the four initiations of the Lesser Mysteries, while the uppermost point represents the "All embracing dominion of the Spirit within... ," i.e. the Individuality.

Most candidates arrive at this point in their journey with imbalances or "blind spots" in their development. This is the period of readjustment that must precede entry into the Greater Mysteries before the "keys" to power may be revealed. If this is not accomplished, all sorts of bizarre behavioral traits may manifest.

At the end of the nineteenth century, England saw the establishment of the Hermetic Order of the Golden Dawn. This great outer vehicle counted among its initiates some of the most famous luminaries of the arts, drama and literature. Despite this, it is perhaps most remembered for the inflated egos that brought the Order to the attention of the non-initiated public in the courtroom during ridiculous legal battles! In-fighting, inflated claims and schisms were the rule of the day. One might point to these "soap operas" and observe that the system of initiation and spiritual advancement did not work. But, perhaps, the correct inference would be that these manifestations occurred precisely because the system was working!

I am convinced that the excessively rapid pace they allowed their candidates to progress through the grades caused most of the problems associated with the historical Golden Dawn. In most cases, it only took candidates a month to get advanced to the next grade! This did not allow the "School of Life" to mature the consciousness of the initiate or the effects of the attunements to be fully realized. Thus, I feel that to jump to the conclusion that the process was not working would be ill advised. Far from evidencing a lack of potency, it is my opinion that these outbreaks of disharmony and ego confirm the power of the process. It wasn't the process that was at fault. The fault lies with the people who failed to properly use the tools they were given.

When we take an attunement, we energize our already existing patterns of automatic response – the imbalanced as well as the more positive, appropriate ones. By observing our life situations and interactions, we can choose to reorder those that don't fit with our image of a true servant of light. To establish the pattern of truth within our consciousness, we should deliberately and consistently image, as clearly as our present state of realization will permit, the new image of the perfected personality.

In the esoteric fraternities, great stress is laid upon teaching about the phenomenon of "projection/integration." Projection is the psychological defense mechanism that attributes cause and assigns the control of our reactions to forces or persons outside of ourselves.

Our present society, it seems, includes a pattern whereby individuals or groups seek to blame others for their problems. This has benefited no one, except perhaps the legal profession! We should remember that when we fail to take responsibility for our own circumstances and reactions, preferring instead to attribute them to the agency of others, we have given our power away. If the Devil or God or "the System" is responsible for our reactions then we are victims and are also slaves!

Projection manifests in the Portal as a pattern of casting blame for our shortcomings and inadequacies on other initiates, teachers and the system. This allows us, we think, not to deal with those actions, responses and thoughts that are reprehensible and therefore unworthy of us as seekers of the Light. But, the energy of these patterns continues to exist.

It is repressed, locked away. We might think of ourselves as a homeowner who throws annoying guests down into the basement of our house! Then we must spend our time and energy standing on the trap door of this cellar as the banished individuals attempt to escape!

When we repress this energy instead of channeling it into more positive responses, it forms complexes and manifests its weeds below the surface of our awareness – in our basement! It does not go away.

Incarnation is like a school. We take classes, but we never get a failing grade. If we do not successfully learn our lessons, we must take the class over again – and again, and again! So, until we learn to deal with these projections, we will see their patterns arise again in our life's experiences and they will continue to drain the energy available for activities of higher transformation and for initiation.

In the ancient mysteries, initiation was often depicted as an after death scenario. Dion

Fortune, in fact, has her heroine, Vivien Le Fay Morgan, state, in the novel *Moon Magic:*

There are two deaths, the death of the body and the death of Initiation. And of these two, the death of the body is the lesser.

Examples of these ceremonies can be found in the so-called "Egyptian Book of the Dead" whose proper name is "The Ritual of the Coming Forth by Day," and also in the various Greek myths concerning Hades, (the place, not the god). In this last we see the soul of the departed (the candidate) approaching the Underworld. She must cross the river Styx, the river of forgetfulness that marks the boundary between the worlds. Once across, the departed would invariably come to a crossroads. Crossroads have always been considered special places. They were sacred to the moon goddess Hecate and it was here that witches were said to dance. In our initiation drama the crossroads offer a choice. The path to the left leads to "Tartarus" or the place of punishment. The path to the right leads to the "Elysian Fields" or the place of reward. While the middle-way was the way of rebirth or the

"Royal Road of Initiation." The choice of the candidate was dependent, first, upon their past life and, second, upon getting permission of the "Guardian of the Ways" – the Dweller on the Threshold.

This figure, which, for a male, was portrayed as a hideous old hag and for a female, by a repulsive, troll-like creature, is the embodiment of all our repressed projections, unworthy attitudes, thoughts and emotions for which we could not take responsibility. Or as Dion Fortune's fictional character, Dr. Taverner, described it, a vision of our naked soul! This figure stands guard at the gate of the Higher Awareness, and until confronted successfully we will not pass. This is our karmic debt. How do we confront the Terror on the Threshold? The old mystery texts advise us that, "fear is failure!" If we turn and run, we close our eyes to possible triumph. What then must we do to enter through the gate and to pass across the threshold guarded by this watcher?

Traditionally the only token that will gain us passage is the embrace of acceptance and love and the kiss of peace. For here is our own shadow! The Terror is the rejected part of ourselves that we must reclaim and redeem so that it may be reintegrated with our total conscious awareness. We must condemn the sin, but not the sinner, realizing that these responses and projections were imperfect, immature reactions, but that they were the best that we could do, given our level of awareness at the time. These lessons must be learned, this wisdom garnered. We must accept our shadow for what it is. And, as in the fairy tales, "The Frog Prince" or "Beauty and the Beast," our shadow will be freed and transformed into a creature of Light. The energy that was trapped in the patterns of repression will be freed, sometimes quite dramatically. This can propel our personality into a quantum leap of illumination. The Dweller has become the vision of our Holy Guardian Angel – our own True Self!

Chapter 45
The Three Tests of the Adept

Life is a gift of abundance. He does not limit our treasure. His gifts are freely given and are, in fact, our Divine birthright! True, the "appearance" of limitation is a necessary illusion while we function in time and space. It helps evolve our consciousness, our awareness of the uniqueness of God's creation through each one of us. But, this is an illusion – a tool for practicing our Divine gift of creativity.

We limit ourselves by buying into the great lies. Lies that have been so insidiously fostered in our consciousness for such a long time. They seem to be verified by experience, although this is because they have become self-fulfilling prophecies. We largely ignore the fact that they are not absolute, they are not "givens;" they are lies. These lies must be conquered before an individual may justly be considered an adept.

On the Tree of Life, entry into the sephirah Tiphareth or "Beauty" symbolizes initiation into the state of consciousness called "adepthood." For Tiphareth represents the "Individuality," the "Christ Consciousness," the "Holy Guardian Angel" and the "Higher Self."

In the symbolism of King Solomon's Temple, Tiphareth represents the Sanctum Sanctorum or "Holy of Holies." In the Masonic legend it is this "Adytum" that is said to be uncompleted. This symbolism is also depicted by the unfinished pyramid on the reverse of the Great Seal of the United States. In this example, we see the capstone descending from heaven to complete the structure. This harkens back to the psalm, where it is stated:

"Except the Lord build the house, they labor in vain who build it."

This is essentially an act of co-creatorship with the Divine.

In the ritualistic practices of the esoteric fraternities, the point of departure for this stage of the journey into Higher Consciousness is said to be the sephirah Yesod, the "Foundation" and our deep consciousness. It is here that the "Bow of Aspiration" launches the "Arrow of Sagittarius" that rends the veil that traditionally separates our personality awareness from the clear perception and eventual identification with the True Self – the Shekinah or Divine Presence.

What must be overcome, what must be transmuted that will allow each of us to penetrate this veil and pass through the portal into the chamber of the Higher Initiation?

Examining the Tree of Life itself reveals the answer to this question. This diagram serves, not only as a training device for the unfolding of consciousness during the process of initiation, but also depicts this process as similar to progress on a map or chart. For this reason, I have chosen to call the diagram illustrated in Figure Four "The Path of the Arrow."

You will also note that the sephirah Yesod, together with the paths of Peh, Ayin, Nun and Samekh can be seen to form a stylized Mars symbol (♂). It is well known that this sephirah, while considered the "Sphere of the Activity of the Moon," has strong connections with Mars energy. This energy is the vehicle for the Cosmic Will Power and is made use of in the activities surrounding reproduction. This also is the energy that provides the fuel and impetus for the illumination process. To act as Its conscious transmitter is the purpose and goal of human personality. It is through the powers of our deep consciousness, the aspect of consciousness specialized in Yesod, that the Cosmic Will reproduces Itself in the kaleidoscope of forms that are so necessary for achieving the goal of the evolution of consciousness. One of the tasks of the initiate is to correct the many erroneous images that are held in this Collective Consciousness. These are images that have been left over from earlier stages of development but are no longer appropriate. Primary among these erroneous images are those outworn attitudes and expressions relating to the reproductive energy. The "dirtiness" that has been associated with it by immature minds must be completely purged from the responses of the aspirant. No matter how sex has been misused in the past, the enlightened attitude that it is, in fact, a sacred expression of the Divine must be thoroughly grounded in the consciousness of the initiate.

The regeneration attributed to this energy never refers to the external organs nor to any trickery connected with the sex act. Rather, it is the Divine Serpent Fire working through the interior centers that is redirected for the spiritual transformation known as the Greater Initiation.

The three paths that form the "arrow head" of our diagram, i.e. the paths of Peh, Ayin, and Nun, designate the great tests of the Three Lies that must be overcome by each aspirant before they can be truly considered an Adept.

The Path of Samekh that forms our "arrow shaft" depicts the key to conquering the illusions of these three great lies.

The First Lie – That of Separation

The Path of Peh has, as one of its attributions, the 16th Key of the Major Arcana of the Tarot, "The Tower," above. It is essentially a picture of a lightning struck castle. Castles were originally tower forts, built on isolated, easily defended hilltops or peaks. Their main function was to provide defense and shelter against an enemy. An enemy or adversary is separate from oneself – a foe, not a friend. Castles or towers were built because of fear of invasions. Fear is the key word here! Yet it is said, "Fear is failure!" This is because fear is based upon the delusion of separateness and it blinds us to the unity of all life.

The Lie of Separation usually manifests in three ways:

[1] The separation of "Inside" and "Outside": This states that the "inside" world (i.e. of consciousness), is fantasy, unreal and that the "outside" world is the only reality. This leads to the idea that the physical may be exploited along with the consequent rape of the environment. Old shamans used to think that their rituals were absolutely necessary to preserve the cosmic balance. In our "enlightened" age, we know this is not true. Now we have acid rain, deforestation of the rain forests and pollution of the oceans! Maybe the shaman was right. Also, this lie leads to the denial of feelings and emotions and the repression of mental states leading to a sterility of consciousness. The truth is that the inner world is the world of cause and the outer reality is its effect. They are not separate but constitute a continuum.

[2] The separation of "self" from "others": This may be simply stated as the "Better Me than Thee!" philosophy. It is the concept that there is only a limited amount of "Good" to go around in the Universe, and if I don't get mine, someone else will get it. This leads to the less noble aspects of competition, the idea that we must gain at the expense of another and that the elevation of the conqueror is at the expense of the vanquished and all others. It contributes as well to war, rape, and crimes of violence and the general victimization of others. And finally, it is a denial of our stewardship of the general welfare.

[3] Separation of "God" and "Man/Woman": The idea of original sin must be balanced by the remembrance of original blessing and godliness. Without this antidote, we see a reinforcement of the distorted image of humanity as a "sinful, worm in the dust," so prevalent during the Middle Ages. This unworthy self-image tends to become a self-fulfilling prophecy. Thus, one who is lacking in worthiness may not become an heir to the Spirit.

The Second Lie – That of Materialism

This lie may be explained by examining the 15th Key of the Major Arcana of the Tarot, above. The name of this Key is "The Devil" which means "The Liar." There are several symbols in its design that point out the fallacy of this lie, which states that the material world is the whole of reality. It would have us believe that what you see in the material universe is all that there is, that all phenomena can be explained by the interaction of matter and sometimes its energetic counterpart.

However, even the best physicists, doing the most advanced work, will tell you that this is an exploded theory! I advise the reader to check out the movie, "What the Bleep Do We Know?" For an entertaining update on the state of Quantum Physics that is relative to this discussion.

Another reference to this lie is revealed in the reverse orientation of the pentagram, featured so prominently in this Key. With the single point of spirit being lower than the four elemental points, it suggests that human beings are at the mercy of elemental forces, outside and beyond their control. The pentagram in its proper orientation, with the spirit point surmounting the four points of the elemental nature, tells quite a different story. It says, the Spirit, which we really are, is the ruler and creator of our world!

The "half cube" throne that supports the central figure symbolically reinforces this idea. A cube, because it looks the same, no matter which surface serves as its base, has traditionally been regarded as a symbol for truth. A half cube, therefore, would suggest a half-truth; perhaps we are only seeing half of the picture. This would confirm that half of the process of manifestation is invisible to one who looks only at the surface play of manifestation. The full picture is reserved for those individuals who have trained themselves to see beneath the surface of the universe.

Finally, you will notice that the chains that bind the human figures to the half cube of bondage are possessed of large loops and could be removed. This represents the truth that the key to freedom is in our own hands, if we would but take control! This control is related to responsibility, as we have mentioned earlier.

The materialist's creed is "He who dies with the most toys, wins!" I would suggest, rather, that "He who dies with the most toys, is still dead!!!" Not a very satisfying outcome.

However, one who adopts as the basis of their philosophy the activity of giving, as heart-felt, freely performed acts of charity, may experience a more rewarding and satisfying life. As it says in an old mystery text, "Charity extends beyond the grave through the realms of eternity."

The Third Lie – That of Mortality

I remember one of my favorite lines from the movie *Contact*. It concerns the question of whether there is other intelligent life in the universe. Jodie Foster's character states, "Well, if there isn't, it is certainly a great waste of space!" The same could be said of the concept of mortality. If the creator of the universe went to all the trouble to create the world and everything in it for a brief one-time run at perfection – what a waste!

The Lie of Mortality is perhaps the most insidious of the three great lies for it has been reinforced by our seeming inability to see beyond the boundaries of this life. By and large, the followers of the mystery traditions subscribe to a belief in reincarnation. This is not as exotic as it would first appear. In reality, the majority of the followers of exoteric religions have also professed this belief at one time or another in their history. Even Orthodox Christianity before the Nicene Council held this belief. And despite the determined effort of the Church to remove every reference to the doctrine of rebirth, there are still plenty of instances in which they failed to do so.

Why did they do this? Because the simple and tragic answer is, it is easier to manage the masses for the benefit of the ruling elite if they think that the rulers hold the keys to eternal reward or damnation in their hands!

The initiate knows otherwise. We return again and again to perfect our expression of God's Power, Wisdom and Love, and to serve our fellows creatures, human and other, life after life. In the Western Tradition, we do not believe that we descend into lower (animal) incarnations. Just because we may act like an ass does not mean we will incarnate as a donkey! (So the donkeys may relax!)

In Tarot Key13, "Death," above, we see the symbolic message of immortality in more than a few places. For example, the sun in the background of the design is assumed, by the uninitiated, to be a setting sun, symbolic of the end of the day. Even if this were true, every sunset is followed by the dawn of a new day. But, according to an ancient tradition, except in a few specific cases, we are told that we view each Tarot Key as if we were facing the direction east! Therefore, the sun we see in this picture is not setting, but is rising! It is thus a symbol of rebirth. Also, the initiate knows that if skin were covering this skeleton it would become immediately obvious that there are two extreme twists in the backbone. One is located in the throat area and the other in the pelvis. It is noteworthy that the pictures of the Egyptian gods and goddesses were always represented this way in ancient Khem!

This apparent deformity refers to a very important lesson regarding the attainment of conscious immortality. It involves a redirection of the energy that is connected with the two interior centers or charkas that are located at these locations. The key to this redirection is found in the symbol of the white rose in the picture. It is a symbol of purified desire!

Most spiritual aspirants have little problem dissociating from identification with the physical body. This is because of their long years of meditation and their development of the powers of the mind. They know they are not their body. However, since most also have pride in their mind's capabilities, it is not as easy to realize that we are also not our mind, emotions or personality. We are not our egos. This requires additional meditative work. Since the personality, and hence the ego, is built up in reaction to the various factors comprising our early environment, family relations and the pressures of our social interactions, it should be obvious that this ever shifting complex of response patterns can have no constancy, no immortality. What then is that part of us that survives life after life? We see our lives strung like the beads upon the necklace of existence; but what is the string that underlies these beads? What is it that is the "I" that survives and gives us identity life from life? If we have attachment to form, to mind, to ego, we are doomed to suffering, the Buddha tells us. And in this the Western adept is in complete agreement.

But many initiates have a memory of the essence of a continuous existence, stretching across the centuries. There is without a doubt, something that has a continuity of consciousness. This something is referred to as the Individuality, the Higher Self or the Holy Guardian Angel. It is this Consciousness that is the vehicle for the evolution just as the personality is the vehicle for the individual incarnation. It is this level that retains the experiences, lessons and capacities that are realized in the long journey of awakening. Yet, this also is not our true self, for it changes also, with the experience of each life. What is that consciousness that sends forth the Individuality to gain the experience of time and space, life after life? There is only one answer and that is the Divine.

The Key to Overcoming the Three Great Lies

"Equilibrium is the secret of the Great Work!"

All of the work in the First Order, with its many lessons, equips the initiate with the capacities and persistent aspiration that is necessary to pass the Tests of the Adept. Remember, the 25th Path, represented by Key 14, "Temperance," is known as the Path of the Intelligence of Probation and Trial. In order to endure the Trials and pass the Tests, the aspirant must have developed the capacity and the strength to sustain his aspiration.

The initiate must seek the correlation between the activities of the personality and Cosmic Cycles. Before the intellect can comprehend this, repeated recollections of this concept must be experienced until all affinity for past inappropriate responses are purged from the center of deep memory, known in the East as the Manipura Chakra, and in our tradition as the Jupiter Center. This interior center, whose physical correlation is the solar plexus, acts as the storehouse of Akashic memory. Many of the responses held there are no longer appropriate for the advanced consciousness the aspirant is striving to develop. They do, however, still have a magnetic attraction because of the quality of inertia, influenced by Race Consciousness. Thus, we may find ourselves slipping into response patterns that belong to a past period of unfoldment.

When the initiate finds himself reacting in a way that is inharmonious with the adept's consciousness he is seeking to embody, he must reject that response and open himself up to the ever present guidance of the illuminated awareness of the Lords of Light. This "inviting of the higher awareness" must be elaborated in all of our daily activities. We must eliminate the bonds of separation that have become a hindrance to our seeking for liberated consciousness. We must make considerable progress in this respect before we are permitted to receive the knowledge of the higher aspects of the Ancient Wisdom. We must have placed our responses under the direction of the Individuality and have demonstrated our consistent discipline in avoiding using of our power to satisfy selfish personal ego needs.

This requires the brutal honesty that we previously described in connection with meeting the Dweller on the Threshold. We transform the excuses, rationalizations and cover-ups that masquerade as spiritual lambs; but, in fact, are the vehicles of the wolves of separation, materialism and other limiting responses.

Thus, we become willing to open ourselves up to receive the higher expression of Grace because we are receptive to the idea that all the energies that flow through us, all the motives that animate us, all the will and love that we express and gives us our sense of individual, personal identity, is not really personal at all – but the expression of the Cosmic Self. We must faithfully and consistently practice the old Rosicrucian vow:

"I will look upon every circumstance of my life as a direct dealing of God with my soul."

Chapter 46
The Greater Mysteries

My weapons were now ready, and the next phase of my career lay with the world ... It was my task to bring certain new concepts to the mind of the race, not to its conscious mind, but to its subconscious mind, and this is done by living them. One who had knowledge once said that an adept must not merely tread the Path, he must be the Path and this is true.

(*Moon Magic* by Dion Fortune)

In the Lesser Mysteries, also called the "Mysteries of Isis," the work was directed toward the perfection and balancing of the individual personality and its vehicles. In the Greater Mysteries, after a period of gaining skill in technique and faculties, the work is directed toward assisting in the work of the Hierarchy in seeding and activating the great centers of power, known as the Archetypes, within the Group Mind of Humanity. This work is done under the direction of those mysterious members of the so-called "Third Order." Many have questioned the existence and reality of these individuals. Apart from my own conviction that these adepts do exist and take an active, if inconspicuous, beneficent interest in the progress of the human race, I would submit the following. For ages, in cultures widely separated, there has been a consistent teaching as to their presence and assistance. Individuals, the world over, have testified to encountering them at critical junctures of our history. Documentary evidence exists testifying to their activities. When such universal evidence supports some phenomenon, it should be taken seriously. I would recommend that the interested reader consult a small book entitled, *The Cloud Upon the Sanctuary,* by Karl von Ekhartshausen, for further enlightening discussion on this subject.

Fictional tales abound with the theme of the cloaked and robed adept who appears in the story at a critical moment, in response to a sincere call for help. He exercises mysterious powers to aid the forces of light and then retires anonymously back to his unknown habitation. Before we consider how an initiate of the Greater Mysteries may assist in the work of these members of the Third Order, let us take a moment to consider what manner of person these higher initiates are.

The noted Tarot and Qabalah expert, the late Dr. Paul Foster Case, tells us of his encounter with a representative of the "Invisible Order." He refers to him simply by the initial "R." In the 1920's, Paul was contacted by this individual on the telephone and invited to meet him face-to-face. The location of this meeting was not a hidden temple or arcane library, high in the remote recesses of the Andes or Himalayan Mountains but in New York City, at the old Waldorf Astoria. The individual met Dr. Case in one of the luxury suites of the hotel. He was not in a cloak or robe but did wear a suit of expensive and tasteful cut. When Paul knocked at the door, "R" himself, not a turbaned servant like those in novels, answered it.

However, having said all this, Dr. Case reported, that when the door was opened, a man who radiated holiness and power met him. Light and love seemed to shine from his eyes. Case introduced himself and started to fall, right in the hallway, to his knees. "R," however, instructed him not to do so. Instead he shook his hand. Case stated that he spent several days in this adept's presence. During this time he described an experience in which he felt his mind being "imparted" or "impacted" with information and knowledge that would take years of work to bring forth. We might use a computer analogy and say that Case's mind received a "download" that would provide "print-outs" for the rest of his life! Case did produce volumes of lessons sourced, he said, from this encounter.

I have no doubt that there are those dedicated individuals of advanced evolution who are concerned with the inner governance of the world. They are not concerned with the outer politics of greed and special interests, but with guiding and equilibrating those secret spiritual influences that rule the minds of those who make up our society. They partner with those initiates who enter incarnation upon the physical plane for the purpose of cooperating with them in the world.

What is the agenda, then, that an initiate of the Greater Mysteries, might be given in order to help humanity? What is the job of the adept and his or her students, now, at the beginning of the third millennium?

First of all, we may be sure it is one of a progressive rather than a conservative philosophy. Paul Foster Case expressed this in the following words:

Finally, the magical will is a power of development, and a dissolving power, also. It is a power, which takes form in mental imagery.... It is a power, which impels him through which it works to be ever on the side of progress. Magicians, therefore, are always among the radicals, not on the side of the conservatives who rely on the power of precedent. Magicians have been the hidden forces at work behind every step in human progress toward the better realization of the ideal of freedom. It is this magical will that has practically overthrown monarchy, which has done so much to change the status of women and children, which is necessarily a perpetual menace to the cant, hypocrisy and formalism of organized external religions.

(2008. *Esoteric Secrets of Meditation and Magic. Volume 2: The Early Writings.* Fraternity of the Hidden Light.)

The Agenda is not secret. We invite all who are willing to help to join with us in accomplishing the following goals:

[1] The reestablishment of balance and harmony in world affairs and relationships between nations. To this end, I have included in the appendices of this book both "The Tower of Light Ritual" and the "Declaratio Lucis."

[2] The rehabilitation of Sacred Sites. This is done through honoring, meditating and visualizing the holy purposes for which the sites were originally constructed.

[3] The recognition of the obligation for the general welfare. We are our Brother's Keeper. While one suffers we all do!

[4] The redemption of sacred archetypes. For example, "The Divine Feminine." We cannot manifest balance in our world as long as we deny one half of it.

[5] The replacement of the negative aspects of competition with those of cheerful cooperation and the win/win model.

[6] The recognition of the inherent right of each individual to practice and hold his or her own beliefs in sacredness and God as long as it does not harm another. (All paths that lead to God are good!) And, for those who so choose, to feel free from expressing any religion whatsoever.

[7] The reclaiming of the essential nobility and worth of each individual.

Finally, it is generally recognized among mystical and sacred psychology circles that we are standing upon the threshold of a major paradigm shift. This shift will be a "quantum leap" in the evolution of consciousness for the human race. Those pledged to aid and assist the members of the Third Order will act as "midwives" to help humanity in the birthing process of this new awakening. "The work is great and the hands are few."

Appendices

Appendix 1

The Tower of Light Ritual

The Tower of Light Ritual was an outcome of the "One Light International Conclave" in 2000. This event, held in Dallas, Texas, was an international symposium (The first of a series) whose purpose was to bring various vehicles of the Western Mysteries into a closer accord of mutual recognition and support.

The ritual was held on the evening of the final day of the event, with officers of all the groups present participating. Its purpose was to promote the influence of the healing light and unity of modern mystery schools in the world.

There are four main officers:

(1) Magus in the East (the Keeper of the Light)
(2) The West (Keeper of the Law)
(3) The South (Keeper of the Way)
(4) The North (Keeper of the Secret)

There are four additional Officers:

(1) The Shower of the Way (a Guide)
(2) A Drummer
(3) The Guardian of the Portal
(4) Warder

The main officers are seated in their respective quarters, facing a central altar. The other officers are stationed as suggested in the ritual.

This ritual is provided here so that the reader may get an idea of the purpose and dynamics of group ritual. The Fraternity invites any group who wishes to perform this ritual to do so with its blessing, so that the stated purpose may be reinforced in the group mind of humanity and become an instrument of the purpose of the Greater Mysteries.

The Ritual

Ritual Requirements

After all have entered, the guardian gives each a small candle. The four chief officers enter carrying implements as follows:

East: Wearing a Yellow Cordelier and carrying a lighted candle and rose

South: Wearing a Red Cordelier and carrying the censor and lamp

West: Wearing a Blue Cordelier and carrying the Cup and Balance Scales

North: Wearing a Black Cordelier and carrying the Paten of Bread and Salt

Guide: Wearing a White Cordelier and carrying a Staff

(Drum plays. All five Chief Officers circumambulate the hall three times. Each time the Guide passes the East, he knocks once, counting the revolutions. On the final circumambulation as each officer reaches his place, the Guide moves to the door. All sit down in unison.)

THE SETTING OF THE WARDS

East: "The Great Wheel of the Heavens turns ever. The Universe continues the Cosmic Dance."

South: "The Divine Plan of Light unfolds."

West: "We come together to redeem the Garden with our Images – such is the Law."

North: "The Secret Oneness: As above, So Below, As Within, So Without. For we are children of the Earth."

All: "But our Race is from the Starry Heavens!"

East: "Let the wards be established."

(The Wards are set by the Warder, using whatever Banishing Ritual has been predetermined to be appropriate.)

PURIFICATION and CONSECRATION

East: "Let the Sanctuary of Light be purified."

West: (Officer of the West advances to the altar and raises the chalice to salute the East, passes North of the altar to the East, circumambulates, sprinkling water as (s)he goes, stopping at the quarters to purify. As he walks, (s)he intones the following):

"The Sea is like the Womb of the Great Lady. From Her the Waters of Life issue forth. To Her all return after the course is run. She is forever pure, forever virgin, forever undefiled."

East: "Let the House of the Holy Fire be consecrated."

South: (Officer of the South adds incense to the censor so that it is actively smoking and proceeds to the altar, raises censor to salute East. Then passes South of the altar to the East, circumambulates, censing as (s)he goes, stopping at the quarters to consecrate. As (s)he walks, (s)he intones the following):

"The Holy Fire transforms all things, for it is a symbol of the Divine Love."

East: (Walking to altar with candle): "Since the misty times of the beginning, the Light has been a symbol for the Spirit. We who are Seekers of this Spirit serve the Light. I hereby place this symbol upon our altar to attest that it is not our work, but the work of the Great Ones: the work of the Hierarchy of Light!"

Officers: (Officer of the East elevates the light and places it upon the altar. All officers rise and together bow to the light on the altar. East returns to station.)

LITANY OF THE QUARTERS

East: "Brother (Sister) Guardian of the North, where is your station within this Sanctuary?"

North: "In the North, Venerable."

East: "Why in the North?"

North: "To guard and keep the Gate of the future."

East: "What is your inner title?"

North: "I am the Keeper of the Secret."

East: "What is your symbol?"

North: "The Hourglass."

East: "What does it symbolize?"

North: "The illusionary and ever-shifting nature of time. When we penetrate the secret of the One Being, we find that Eternity is the cause of the past, present and future."

East: "Let this symbol be placed upon the altar so that it may be known that the Powers it represents are operating in this Sanctuary."

Guide: (Goes to the North, takes the hourglass to altar and places it north of the Light already there.)

East: "Brother (Sister) Guardian of the South, where is your station within this Sanctuary?"

South: "In the South, Venerable."

East: "Why in the South?"

South: "To guard and keep the Gate of Remembrance."

East: "What is your Inner title?"

South: "I am the Keeper of the Way."

East: "What is your symbol?"

South: "The Lamp."

East: "What does it symbolize?"

South: "The Light of Divine Wisdom and the Ancient Tradition of Initiation."

East: "Let this symbol be placed upon the altar so that it may be known that the Powers it represents are operating in this sanctuary."

Guide: (Places lamp on altar as with hourglass but south of the light.)

East: "Brother (Sister) Guardian of the West, where is your station within this Sanctuary?"

West: "In the West, Venerable."

East: "Why in the West?"

West: "To guard and keep the Gate of Consciousness."

East: "What is your Inner Title?"

West: "I am the Keeper of the Law."

East: "What is your symbol?"

West: "The Scales of Justice – The Balance of Maat."

East: "What does it symbolize?"

West: "The Mystery of Causation – the Truth of the inner origin of creation."

East: "Let this symbol be placed upon the altar so that it may be known that the Powers it represents are operating in this Sanctuary."

Guide: (Goes to West, takes the scales to altar and places them west of the light.)

THE THREEFOLD ADORATION

(Part 1)

All: (Stand.)

South: "Holy art Thou, Father Most Glorious!
      Holy art Thou, Giver of Life!
      Holy art Thou, Seed of our Godhead!
      Thou conquering Victor in Battle and Strife!"

All: (Sit.)

East: "Brother (Sister) of the North, why do I sit in the East?"

North: "To guard the Gate of the Dawning, Venerable."

East: "Brother (Sister) of the West, what is my esoteric title?"

West: "Keeper of the Light, Venerable."

East: "And what is my symbol, Brother (Sister) of the South, and what does it symbolize?"

South: "Your symbols are the Light and the Rose. The Light symbolizes the guidance of the Divine and of the Hierarchy. It has been placed first upon the altar, for no convocation of the Mysteries may truly function without this contact. The Rose is a symbol of Love and the Human Soul. This flower of the Soul opens to the Light within. Only God may unfold this blossom of Light!"

East: "Let those symbols also be placed upon the altar." (Done as before.)

THREE-FOLD ADORATION
(Part 2)

All: (Stand.)

East: "Holy and Blessed, Male-Female Power! Holy and Blessed, this Union Divine! Holy and Blessed, its Joy and its Rapture! One without Second, the True Androgyne!"

All: (Sit.)

East: "By and through the authority invested in us by our dedication to the Light, I hereby declare this Sanctuary an abode of Power, Wisdom and Love, and open for the work of the Great Ones!"

All: "And so it is!"

(CONCLUSION OF OPENING)

* * *

THE OPUS

East: "We have not come together by accident, but by Divine Appointment. In the time before the beginning, we gathered together and made an agreement to meet in solemn convocation to aid in this Great Work – the full manifestation of the Light!"

THREE-FOLD ADORATION
(Part 3)

All: (Stand.)

West: "Blessed art Thou, Mother of Beings! Blessed art Thou, Grace from Above! Blessed art Thou, Virgin and Matron! Thou seat of all Wisdom, Mercy and Love!"

All: (Sit.)

East: "My Brothers and Sisters, in the beginning of creation, when Space and Time were created, the Divine Consciousness established Four Watch Towers and placed them at the boundaries of the Space-Time Continuum. He placed in each of these one of the Great Watchers to guard the Cosmos. Also, He placed a fifth Tower, a Tower of Light that was placed at the Center of All Creation – the center of your heart! Always present, at all times and all space – a Tower of Eternity! Here, He placed a special Watcher – one who was intimately connected with the achievement of the Great Transmutation – the Work of the Triumph of the Divine Power, Wisdom and Love!"

"Some say that this Tower's physical representation existed on Earth in the misty recesses of the Ancient Past. But, one thing is certain; it has always existed on the bright, shining plane of the Spirit!"

"My Brothers and Sisters let these images arise in your consciousness:"

"On a vast, wind-blown, barren, high plane, there exists a tall, ancient stone tower. Nobody knows how long it has been here – it seems like always. It can be seen from anywhere on this vast plateau."

"It has been said, that in times of great need, great crisis or great opportunity, a light shines forth from the Crown of this Tower, and is visible throughout the Kingdom. Its healing illumination shines even into the underworld – even unto the Seventh Step."

"We approach this tower and see a door, an ancient oaken affair, studded with iron spikes. Immediately, we notice that there is no latch or pull to open the door on this side. In the place we would normally expect to find them, there is only a round, brass plaque, approximately seven inches in diameter. One of our number steps forward and with her right forefinger, traces the symbol of the five-pointed, upright star. Immediately, the door dissolves as light, giving each of us free passage within."

"We file into a stone-walled, square-shaped room with a flagstone pavement. In the middle of each quarter is a high-backed throne, also made of gray stone. An altar is situated in the center, once again carved from living stone."

"Our destination is not this tower temple, however, and we proceed to the Northeast corner, where we find stairs leading to the floor above as a drum sounds once from somewhere unseen."

"As we emerge onto the second floor, we are surrounded by an ancient library. On all sides, we see an endless labyrinth of shelves, holding books of all types and ages, as well as tablets of stone and wax, and scrolls of papyrus and leather and leaves. Each bookcase is carved with arcane symbols. The floor, we note, is paved with octagonal tiles inscribed with alchemical, astrological and other esoteric devices."

"Upon the ceiling are depictions of the four seasons with spring to the East, Summer to the South, Autumn in the West and finally, Winter placed in the North."

"We wind our way among the archives as a drum sounds twice, to find a crystal staircase in the Southwest that leads to the third level. We climb the 22 steps, in three series of 7, with a rainbow of colors repeating 3 times. The top step is of clear crystal."

(Drum sounds twice.)

"We emerge onto the third level, a level that is in stark contrast to the one below, for this floor has no furniture or symbols, save for a central cubical altar of the purist white alabaster. Upon this altar burns a light – a light with a steady, unwavering flame. A flame that has shone forth unto the farthest reaches, the very limits of time and space and beyond. Seven windows open out on this level – all without glass or covering. From here, one may magically see Infinity, both future and past."

"We see at one of these windows, gazing steadfastly, silently out on the vista without, an ancient being with white hair and beard, clothed in a long, gray robe. He does not turn to acknowledge us and as yet we choose not to disturb this Watcher of Eternity."

(Drum sounds three times.)

"We center our attention instead upon the flame burning upon the altar. We understand that this manifestation of the Limitless Light is the very embodiment of Perfect Wisdom, Unlimited Power and Unconditional Love – forever balanced, forever united. Its glow consecrates this level and all of creation. We indeed stand upon holy ground. And in recognition, we remove our shoes from off our feet."

"Our purpose is clear. We are here to become bearers of this One Light. We remember the candles we hold and as we hear the beat of the Cosmic Drum, we follow our guide in the special Dance of Light!"

Drummer: (Drummer starts to beat a steady Boom-Boom-Boom cadence with accent on the third of three close beats. Guide begins leading participants in a clockwise spiral to altar. After lighting candle, each participant spirals out in a counter-clockwise path)

Note: Care should be taken to leave space between lines for safe movement. Also, the guide should make sure participants can return to approximately the same position as when they started. Additional ushers might be used. At the end, all participants should be holding small, lighted "vigil" candles.

* * *

<u>CLOSING</u>

East: "Behold, the Watcher turns and smiles upon each of you. He speaks to us:"

"Hail oh Children of Noble Purpose! Behold all of Creation is blessed and healed by your consecrated actions. As you now blow your candle out, extinguish not the light, but take it into the temple of your heart so that it may shine forth ever more brightly as a beacon of Truth, Love and Healing to all the World."

[All now blow candles out.]

East: "May you rest under the shadow of His wings, whose name is peace."

"Before the mists of Time we agreed to come together, each to do their part, their duty to assure the completion of the Great Transmutation. Fulfill your destiny!"

(All Principal Officers stand and walk to the Altar. Together they retrieve their symbols and walk again to their stations. The Eastern Officer, to the cadence of the Drumbeat, circumambulates three times counter-clockwise. He ends up close to the altar facing east. He extinguishes the light upon the altar with the snuffer and says):

"It is finished!"

Appendix 2

Commentary on the Tower of Light Ritual

The Tower of Light Ritual was first performed at the "One Light International Conclave of Mystery Schools" in October, 2000. We desired it to be non-sectarian in form because of the diverse backgrounds of the participants. Its purpose was to express unity and inclusiveness among the various groups of the Tradition. It was further envisioned that this should be a united ceremonial statement of cooperation and mutual support by all those of the esoteric mystical movement.

The story of its creation is noteworthy. Early in 1999, I began to receive various parts of the formula during dreams and deeper meditative experiences. Significantly, others in our Fraternity, notably Soror L:. V:. also began to receive information via the inner planes. None of us had communicated to each other any of these events or the information we had been receiving until almost a year later.

Despite this, when we compared notes, we found that, not only were we in agreement, but that the different parts fit together like an orchestrated dance! Quite clearly, the Inner School was interested in this project going forward.

Further, the intuitional promptings to name the conference the "One Light – 2000" came to members of the Dallas, Texas Temple who had no knowledge that the symbol of the "single light" would be so critical to the working of the ceremony.

The primary symbol came through as a three tiered tower with description much as is found in the finished presentation. Only later, after I had conducted a number of seminars and workshops that included the three-world system prevalent in the mystery traditions of East and West, was the detail about the three levels received. This was through three separate individuals in the Fraternity, during deep meditations – at three different geographical locations.

In the tower we find the first floor with its stone, elemental quarters, etc. as a perfect analogy for the "Soma", "Guph" or "Body" level. Another correspondence could relate to the subconsciousness of the individual but this is not as complete.

It is apparent that the physical temple arrangement with the four thrones and the central altar and light are intended as a reflection of this level of the tower. The image in the tower, of course, represents the astral counterpart of the physical layout of the hall where the ceremony is worked.

The second or middle floor of the tower relates to the "psyche," "Ruach/Nephesh" or level of the Mind. Here we see the "treasure house of images" with the many instances of symbols. This level has been found to be particularly appropriate in accessing what is commonly called the Akashic Records. This symbolic structure can be used as a "jumping off" place to contact the symbolic chain to contact the memory of nature. I will leave it to the reader's imagination how this elaboration might be implemented.

The third level is representative of the "Pneuma, Neshamah, or Spirit" level. Hence it is open on all sides to the Universe, or the Macrocosm. Here we see little symbolic embellishment with the exception of the cubic altar of truth with the flame of Spirit burning upon it.

At this level we encounter the "Watcher." He is dressed and has the appearance that has come to be associated with Tarot trump #9, "The Hermit." And, in this regard, I would urge the reader to study what Paul Foster Case has to say about this design in his book, *Tarot: Key to the Wisdom of the Ages,* published by Macoy.

Besides the attributions already discussed we might also want to considerer the correlations of the four worlds of the Qabalist with the levels of the tower. The four worlds relate directly if we assign the Light of Truth, shining upon the altar on the third level, to the fourth world of Atziluth. The remaining three worlds then correlate as follows:

Briah – the level of the Watcher
Yetzirah – the Library of the Cosmos
Assiah – The Stone Temple

In the "Tower of Light" ritual, the symbolism is calculated to bring the archetypal energy of Unity, Love, Healing and Wisdom into the manifest world through the agencies of the various dedicated organizations of the Mysteries in a united effort.

Appendix 3

Declaratio Lucis

To serve the Limitless Light and travel the Path of Return for its own sake; To labor at the Great Work and become a conscious assistant of Evolution on all levels; To unveil the Mysteries of Nature that one's service will be guided by Truth; To reawaken the proper degree of respect for the precious miracle of Life regardless of the form it inhabits; That one might rise from the ashes of darkness and ignorance to take wing with the Phoenix into the Spiritual Sun; This is the Ideal of the Task to which we have set ourselves and the goal of our purpose.

We do reaffirm the Universal Reformation of Humanity as declared in the older manifestos of the Tradition. To restore, preserve and enlarge those ancient mystical and philosophical systems of initiation, by which humanity will be inclined toward a state of mutual understanding and spiritual integrity. The extension and perfection of all the Arts, by which the power of beauty may be released as a civilizing force. The reconstitution of states toward a philosophic commonwealth whereby the illusion of competition and separateness will be dispelled by the reality of independent co-operation. The creation among the learned of a permanent organization dedicated to essential advancement, devoted to all branches of useful knowledge and capable of providing a perpetual incentive for human progress. The accomplishment of all change without such revolutions as endangers the life and property of the private citizen. The principal instrument of improvement is education. The wise one cannot be enslaved, and the ignorant one cannot be freed.

A New Order of Ages has blessed us with a Golden Dawn. A Tradition of ritual and ideal born from the Limitless Light of Being. A map of the labyrinth to guide us to the Inmost and Most High. The Lie of Separateness has held the Human Race in its grip since before the time of Imperial Rome. Many have succumbed to its subtle seductiveness. Even our own Tradition has suffered this taint and yet the Diaspora of its illumination continues to blossom. The time is upon us for a real, conscious, sustained effort to join together as One, to put the Great Work first, before the origin or pedigree of a particular vehicle or the grade of one's attunement. Ours is a Path that quits this Night of Materialism for an Unreserved Dedication to the Light – a dedication of service to all Life.

Such is the Oratory of our hearts and the Laboratory of our hands and mind.

For

The Hermetic Light is Truth and Wisdom.

* * *

The Declaratio Lucis, or Declaration of Light, was received meditatively by members of the Fraternity of the Hidden Light just prior to "The One Light World Conclave," in Dallas Texas, in 2000 A.D. It was conceived as a statement of intent and a pattern of conduct for the New Millennium. Over a dozen major esoteric vehicles of the Western Tradition and thousands of sincere aspirants have adopted it.

If you would like to receive a free copy on parchment, with suitable seals, communicate with the author at: Fraternity of the Hidden Light, P.O. Box 5094, Covina, California, U.S.A., 91723

Appendix 4

Pathworkings

I have included two sample pathworkings so that the reader can get some idea of what they are. You can find additional good examples in many of the works by Dolores Ashcroft-Nowicki. In the Fraternity, these are considered to be deep, guided meditations in some cases and exploratory meditations in others. Upon some occasions, initiates have been placed in a light trance and then led through a particular working in the days following their more formal ceremonial work, related to the same path, in order to integrate the experience more thoroughly in their consciousness.

The Path of the Sun or the letter Resh

Prepare yourself and your sanctum as usual. Let these images arise in your consciousness:

The Temple of Yesod builds up around me. I see the stardust floor, the silver and black pillars, the white altar with its silver bowl and lotus flame. I see also that the Archangel Gabriel awaits me. Standing with him is a youth, somewhat shorter than he. This youth bears golden wings and upon his chest, a golden sun disk is strung upon a golden chain.

Gabriel introduces his companion: "This is Mikal, the Angel of the Sun. I have asked him to act as your guide as you travel the Path of Resh."

"Greetings, oh aspirant. Thank you for allowing me to share in your initiatory adventure. For, as you know, we may not advance in our evolutionary quest save through devoted service to the Creator and each other. My realm is the 30th Path of the letter Resh – the Path of the Sun. It is called in your ancient writings the 'Path of the Collective Intelligence,' for the energies you contact in this aspect of the One is the power that resides at the center of each of you. It is the power that finds expression in your manifested universe as the sun. And remember – this is the power of a great consciousness. The sun is the physical vehicle of the Solar Logos! Thus, it was only right, in ages past, that humankind expressed recognition of these facts. Let us enter the Path of the Sun and attend such a ceremony."

We walk to the door in the southeast corner of the Temple. Gabriel traces the letter "Resh" before it thus:

ר

The door begins to vibrate and dissolves into an orange mist. This mist resolves into the vision of torchlight. I find I am standing on a vast antediluvian plain. It is in the hour before dawn. I am walking in a line of dark-robed initiates. We are walking down a procession way lined with sphinxes with the heads of rams. I look up the line and see that we are marching towards a stone circle, much like the famous Stonehenge on the Salisbury Plain. This one is, however, new and complete; although I know Stonehenge only as the ruined remains of today. As we near the circle, we start spiraling inward, clockwise toward the center. Round and round we go. The feeling of power grows as we make this strange journey.

Finally we stop. Each one of us now faces the middle of the ring with one of the giant monoliths behind us. There is an altar at the center of the circle and, upon this altar is a huge topaz! Only in this realm of magic could a gem this large exist. Or could it exist in other, more physical planes of manifestation? Am I limiting the power of my imagination – the gift of the sun?

There is a hush of expectation, of anticipation, as we all face the increasing rose glow upon the horizon. As the solar disk bursts into view, the entire congregation of robed priests and priestesses burst forth into song:

Holy art Thou, Oh God, the Father of the Universe!
Holy art Thou, Oh God, whose will perfects itself by means of its own powers.

Holy art Thou, Oh God, who willest to be known and art known by Thine own.
Holy art Thou, Who didst by Word make to exist the things that are.
Holy art Thou, of whom all nature hath been made an image!

Then, with our arms outstretched in exultant adoration, we see a ray from the sun strike directly into the heart of the topaz upon the altar. From this stone, the light is refracted and multiplied in brilliance. Its glory seems to encompass me; and within the vision, I experience this vision:

From the flash of light I am plunged into total darkness! I am floating in a velvety dark void of blackness. Nowhere is there any light – but wait – yes – deep within me I see a glowing spark, pulsing with every heartbeat. As I direct my attention to this ember, this jewel of light, it begins to expand and increase in brilliance with each breath. The light within continues to grow until it extends out past me. I am a glowing center of light, spinning through this dark expanse of space! I am a star! A sun! I give out light, overcoming the darkness. I am the light shining in the night of time. The light that the darkness cannot conquer! Now I notice a small spherical object. A lonely lump of clay, revolving, orbiting about me in the darkness. The planet earth! Frozen, barren, lifeless; it calls to me, and is part of me. A wave of compassion floods my being and I reach out with a ray of my light and bathe this globe with love. Almost immediately, it begins to awaken from its icy sleep and plants begin to bud. Life is born. I witness the flowering of creation.

Now, once again, I am standing before the topaz in the circle. The sun is now a little above the horizon. A voice from within speaks to me as I close my eyes:

Behold the Jewel of eternity!
From the Source came you forth,
Robed in the Garment of Light,
Dancing the Dance of Return,
Swaying with the rhythm of the Cosmos,
Spreading healing from beneath your wings.
Enter, my child the moment of forever --
For the Light of Illumination

Descends not from above,
But from within!

When I open my eyes, I find that I am again in the Temple of Yesod, looking into the eyes of the Angel of the Sun. Gabriel is sealing the portal of Resh. Mikal says, "Welcome back. You now bear, consciously, a link with the Collective Intelligence." He presents me with a solar disk upon a chain. In the center is a small topaz. "Bear this jewel within your heart, and remember the Love that unites us all." The Temple and the two angelic beings fade as I once again become more aware of my physical surroundings.

Perform the "earthing" exercise. Enter the experience in your journal.

*   *   *

The second pathworking selected is one of the more important ones. It is attributed to the 6th sephirah, "Tiphareth," the Sphere of the Sun, and the entry point for the Greater Mysteries. Also, since it deals with a sephirah rather than an interconnecting path, certain differences should be noted.

The Temple of the Sun

My eyes are closed and I am cold. I try to let the senses other than sight give me information about my whereabouts and conditions before I open my eyes. It is cold, as I have said, and damp. In fact, I hear the dripping of moisture not too far from me. I am lying on my back upon a hard, stone surface. The wind whistles and sings a sad lament. Every so often I feel its draft. When I finally open my eyes, I find that I am looking up at a vaulted ceiling made of ancient stonework. It is quite dark; the only illumination is provided by torchlight. Spider webs occupy the corners where the arches meet the roof of this chamber.

I turn my head to the side to gain a better perspective of my surroundings and realize that I am staring eye-to-eye with a skeleton. It is quite close, no more than nine inches away. The empty sockets gazing back at me seem to hold its secrets intact. The skeleton is lying next to me on a cold burial slab. It is clothed in the rags of a dress, the burial shroud, most of it having lost the war with decay. I turn my head to the other side and find a similar figure, not so far into decomposition, this one clothed in the armor of a warrior!

I sit up and look around. Yes, all around I see sepulchers, coffins and bones. I am in a burial vault. And I am ready to leave these melancholy precincts! I see a door at the top of a stairway on the other side of the vault. I get up and slide to the floor, trying to avoid disturbing the remains of my present companions. As I make my way toward the door, something stirs in the shadows around the door – something large. I freeze in my tracks. A hiss of steam colored by two red, glowing eyes heralds the wedge-shaped reptilian head as it rises and focuses it baneful gaze upon me. Its tail starts to move, slowly at first, like a serpent, but then twitches back and forth, like a great cat's. From out of legends this great black dragon uncoils from its slumber and blocks the door – the only exit from this dark vault of mortality!

I silently invoke the One Source and visualize a golden cross between the beast and myself. Then a glowing point of light rapidly expands, becoming a mighty warrior figure – a warrior of light! He is dressed in golden armor, holding a golden shield with the emblem of the Sun blazoned upon it. In his other hand he holds a flaming sphere. With this he subdues the black serpent and places his foot upon its head. "Come," he says. "For those who invoke the Light with a pure heart, there is always safe passage over the black dragon!"

I hurry up the stairs and accompany him through the door. I find myself in a small temple of pure, white stone. Inlaid in gold and silver upon the floor is a giant hexagram, with the triangle of gold pointing away from me, interlaced with the one of silver, whose apex points directly at the entrance within which I now stand. In the exact center of this temple, beneath a golden lamp, hanging from a chain, is an altar. This altar is of the purest white alabaster and is in the shape of a perfect cube, 26 inches to a side. On top of this altar, standing upright and revolving clockwise so that it is first facing East, then South, West and then North, is a golden pentagram, sparkling in the light.

My guide takes off his helmet, revealing a young man with red hair and beard and startling blue eyes. He regards me steadily: "I am Michael, the Archangel of the Sun. Welcome to the Temple of the Mediating Influence – the hall of your own Higher Self!" With this he breaks into a smile. "The vault of the black dragon is the only way into this adytum. It is by disintegrating and transmuting the force he represents that we are reborn into Truth. Solve et Coagula – dissolve and reform – transmute and sublimate!"

"Humanity is uniquely the Mediating Intelligence. For the Spirit you really are is the channel through which the energies represented by Jacob's ladder passes up and down the planes. We of the Angelic evolutions possess only faculties of the worlds of Briah and Yetzirah. Our little brothers and sisters of the Elemental Kingdom are limited also. They are of Assiah and Yetzirah only. Humanity alone possesses all three and can thus direct the energies for the Great Transmutation, the great redemption."

Michael reaches to the altar and stops the spinning pentagram. He picks it up and places it, single point uppermost, upon my heart. "Take the Lamen of the Pentalpha and wear it above your heart center. You truly are the star of five rays; for the pentagram symbolizes the dominion of your spirit, the Divine Spirit, over the elemental creation."

"Come now to the Eastern door – the door to the Great Consciousness – and wait in silence!"

He stations me facing a red doorway. It has no handle, no means of gaining admission from this side. Clearly, here is a door that must be opened from within! I wait and watch until the silence and anticipation grows to almost unbearable proportions. The redness of the door is now turning to a bright, bright, shining gold. Its coloring and texture is changing to a mist, a golden mist – no wait – other colors are appearing. A rainbow of colors! I feel myself moving through this rainbow mist to a great light beyond. The light is coming from a stone sarcophagus. Something is rising from it! A beautiful child, seated upon a lotus – a lotus of pure light! The child is holding his left forefinger to his smiling lips. In the other open palm, he is offering me a small truncated pyramid of white. At its summit is a jewel of brightness. The child speaks one phrase – a sentence – into my heart. I hear it, but do I understand? The light encompasses me!

I now take a moment, as the child and inner sanctum fade, to reorient myself with my physical surroundings. My Tiphareth path working is concluded.

For Information on the Fraternity of the Hidden Light or an Application for Probationary Membership:

Visit our website at http://www.lvx.org

Selected References

Clark, Paul A. *The Broken Seal and Other Cases*. Covina, California: Fraternity of the Hidden Light, 2008.

Fortune, Dion. *The Secrets of Doctor Taverner*. With introductory essay on "The Work of a Modern Occult Fraternity" by Gareth Knight. Woodbury, MN: Llewellyn Publications 1971 (1962).

The *Training & Work of an Initiate*. Foreword by Gareth Knight. San Francisco, California: Red Wheel/Weiser, LLC, 2000 (1967 Society of Inner Light).

Aspects of Occultism. Newburyport, MA: Red Wheel/ Weiser, 2000.

The Mystical Qabalah. Newburyport, MA: Red Wheel/ Weiser, LLC, 2000.

Moon Magic. Newburyport, MA: Red Wheel/ Weiser, LLC, 2003.

Gray, William G. *Magical Ritual Methods.* Cheltenham, England: Helios, 1988.

Levi, Eliphas. *Key to the Mysteries*, London, England: Rider & Co., 1959. Translated by Aleister Crowley.

Talbot, Michael. *The Holographic Universe: The Revolutionary Theory of Reality.* New York, London, Toronto, Sydney: Harper Perennial, 2011.

Three Initiates. *The Kybalion: A Study of the Hermetic Philosophy of Ancient Egypt and Greece.* Chicago, Illinois: The Yogi Publication Society, 1940 (1912).

www.ingramcontent.com/pod-product-compliance
Lightning Source LLC
Chambersburg PA
CBHW020634300426
44112CB00007B/114